Orchestrating Supply Chain Opportunities

Orchestrating Supply Chain Opportunities

Achieving Stretch Goals Efficiently

Ananth Iyer and Alex Zelikovsky

First published in 2011 by
Business Expert Press, LLC
222 East 46th Street, New York, NY 10017
www.businessexpertpress.com

ISBN-13: 978-1-60649-223-9 (paperback)

ISBN-13: 978-1-60649-224-6 (e-book)

DOI 10.4128/9781606492246

A publication in the Business Expert Press Supply and
Operations Management collection

Collection ISSN: 2156-8189 (print)
Collection ISSN: 2156-8200 (electronic)

Cover design by Jonathan Pennell
Interior design by Scribe Inc.

First edition: March 2011

10 9 8 7 6 5 4 3 2 1

Printed in Taiwan

Abstract

This book provides a *flexibility, agility, real options* (FAR) framework to orchestrate supply chain opportunities. Using best-practice cases across the industry spectrum, from nonprofits to retail, from demand surges to regulatory impacts and natural disasters, orchestrating supply chain opportunities requires deliberate management choices. This book provides a primer for success.

Keywords

supply chain management, real options, flexibility, agility, ecommerce, disasters, opportunities

Contents

Preface

Companies operate best with efficient planning and superior execution based on clear objectives. For many companies, the planning process is carefully orchestrated, objectives are set, budgets are negotiated, resources are allocated, and then it's up to the organization to execute. But what happens when the unexpected occurs? Say an event occurs that throws the status quo into turmoil. If your business declines by 40% in 1 month, what do you do? Conversely, what if your demand spikes by 50% in just a few months? Suppose a natural disaster happens or a new technology creates a significant but unplanned opportunity? We call these events "stretch opportunities." Our focus is on orchestrating these supply chain opportunities.

Current business challenges include significant shifts in product volumes and customer preferences; global industry shifts that affect manufacturers and distributors; environmental regulations; government-sponsored bailouts; new technologies that revolutionize products; mass customization; and catastrophic climate effects and wild economic swings, to name a few. What do all of these drivers of change have in common? We suggest that all of them can be viewed as "events" that offer significant "stretch opportunities." In every case we researched for this book, there was a short window of opportunity in which a company was able to attain a significant advantage. As these events are inevitable, the key question becomes, how should a company position itself to capitalize on such stretch opportunities?

This book will focus on strategic thinking and tactical examples of how best to prepare for such events. We will outline common themes across all such challenges. We will introduce three key management concepts: *flexibility*, *agility*, and *real options* (FAR). We will present several unique cases illustrating how companies have orchestrated stretch opportunities. The Amazon.com story describes a significant growth opportunity in the early days of e-commerce that occurred during the Christmas peak season. The Reflect.com/Procter & Gamble (P&G) story talks about challenges of mass customization and how innovative solutions leveraged the power of a rapidly emerging e-channel. The U.S. Coast Guard's story describes the response to a natural disaster, demonstrating the power of flexible asset allocation, planning, training, and execution. The Kryptonite story describes the company's rapid recovery from a horrific event that caused a product demand collapse and widespread loss of consumer confidence in the Kryptonite brand. The story of Watsco Inc. shows how a distributor, driven by environmental regulation, reacted to a highly volatile period of demand during product transitions. The United Nations Joint Logistics Center (UNJLC) story shows how a global organization can improvise and adopt relief efforts in an emergency, reconfiguring available resources to meet extreme global challenges. Finally, we will discuss emerging technologies and innovative software solutions that allow companies to be more flexible and more agile, thus offering real options to take advantage of stretch opportunities.

In addition to these real examples, we will take the reader on a fictitious journey of a CEO, Max Zen, and his company, Gizmo Inc. The Max Zen story is the narrative of a company that was rocked by many different events, was able to adopt and overcome unexpected challenges, and leveraged FAR to not only succeed but grow exponentially.

Finally, we provide a chapter on how to structure supply chains to capitalize on stretch opportunities, that is, to build FAR into a supply chain. We will end with a checklist that managers can use to ensure that the right questions are asked in developing supply chains so that the ability to "surge" at profitable opportunities is nourished.

What's New?

Fact: Efficient planning and superior execution based on clear objectives is the way companies operate best. For many companies, the planning process is carefully orchestrated: Objectives are set, budgets are negotiated, resources are allocated, and then it's up to the organization to execute. But what happens when the unexpected occurs? Say an event throws the status quo into turmoil. What if business declines by 40% in 1 month or demand spikes by 50% in just a few months? Suppose a natural disaster happens or a new technology emerges that creates a significant but unplanned opportunity? We call these events "stretch opportunities." This book focuses on orchestrating supply chain opportunities that enable such stretch goals to be attained, efficiently.

Extraordinary Times

We live in extraordinary times. In fact, the 21st century will—not might—bring *unprecedented change* to the way we live. This change will be more radical than all the advances combined in human history. Case in point: Take a simple laptop. An 18-year-old now has more computing processing power at his or her fingertips than our entire nation had about 40 years ago. We are making incredible advances in science, medicine, and technology.

But, of course, change brings enormous challenges. The *speed of change is difficult to comprehend* and impossible to control. Just think: A third of the planet's population is still living on less than $5 per day.

What does the future hold for these emerging global markets? There is only one common denominator in our lives: big changes. Here are a few specific changes that will affect supply chains: significant shifts in product volumes and customer preferences, global industry shifts that affect manufacturers and distributors, environmental regulations, government-sponsored bailouts, new technologies that revolutionize products, mass customization, catastrophic climate effects, and wild economic swings. What do all of these drivers of change have in common?

Recent News Factoids

Before you begin this journey, here are a few facts: Production volumes dropped by 60% from January 2008 to January 2009 in the U.S. auto industry. The cost to ship a container from South China to Europe dropped from $4,000 in 2008 to close to zero in 2009. Over 50% of the toy exporters in China disappeared, and an estimated 70,000 factories were shuttered and over 20 million people left unemployed as a result in 2009. When demand shifts these days, the shift is significant: a 60% drop in global demand for a retail hardware products company; a drop in revenues to 10% of normal for a media company; an upswing of 30% for a beauty products company; a merger between a software and a (primarily) hardware company with significantly different cultures; and disappearing airlines, banks, and retailers. Imagine the impact of these changes worldwide. Clearly the world of physical goods flow and order flow can expect to be hit by such wild capacity and demand shifts repeatedly.

Supply Chain Stretch Opportunities

In every case we researched for this book, there was a short window of opportunity in which a company was able to attain a significant advantage. Because these events are inevitable, the key question becomes, how should a company position itself to capitalize on such stretch opportunities?

Netflix CEO Reed Hastings talks about staying flexible to survive and grow. He claims that the company was named Netflix because it was not clear how long DVDs would be the medium and when movies through the Internet would be a reality. He also claims that it was unclear to Netflix how competitive a threat Blockbuster (which invested more than $500 million over 4 years) would be. But he too claims that the best one can do is build an organization that can offer the potential to seize opportunities as they arise.

There are *opportunities amid change*. A *Fortune* magazine interview with Jeff Immelt and A. J. Lafley—CEOs of General Electric and P&G, respectively—discusses how each of them plans to add $16 billion and $6 billion, respectively, in new revenues each year to their companies.[1] They described innovation, new markets, new products, and new approaches to deliver products as key capabilities to deliver this growth. A *Business Week* article reports that 65 of the top 100 company CEOs expect dramatic changes in their companies in the next 5 years. What kind of changes? How large? When should we expect them? How can we plan and prepare? These are challenges faced by managers across companies. Successful companies seize the opportunity.[2]

Witness the growth in volume at Craftmaster, a furniture company that has grabbed new customers, merged with weak competitors, and capitalized on flexible execution to thrive. Shipping companies adjusted their cruising speed to trade off fuel costs for delivery lead times and lowered their operating costs by more than $1 billion to become competitive. Companies increased their use of information technology tools to reduce physical travel and monitoring. Even the federal government managed to eliminate over $100 million in costs within 90 days. Companies are busy grabbing new customers, merging, streamlining, and building the muscle to compete.

The Concept of FAR

How a company can manage such volatility—strategic thinking and tactical examples of how best to prepare for such events—is the focus of this book. The management guru Jim Collins, interviewed in *Fortune*, discusses how companies survive in turbulent times. He starts by stating that the last 50 years of the last century was remarkable for its stability by any standards of history. His recommendation? "In times of great uncertainty, you have to have moorings. You need to preserve them over time."[3] We agree but would like to be more specific.

Our suggestion is that these moorings have to be embedded in a strategy that enables companies to expand or contract with the times. We will start with six business cases, each of which involved significant business shifts, and then introduce three key management concepts: *flexibility*, *agility*, and *real options (FAR)*. We will show how the management of operations in each of these companies can be interpreted as the successful use of FAR. Our approach—FAR—provides a stretch capability like a rubber band. By structuring a company to take advantage of new growth and new products and by exercising real options, a new dynamic emerges.

Our Book

Our goal in this book is to describe some *heroic successes* and outline how to nurture, prepare, and execute in such contexts. In this book, we will tell you stories of how real companies were able to adapt to large and unexpected changes and succeed. We will help today's business leaders position their respective organizations to meet stretch goals and take advantage of unexpected opportunities. We will not only help you ask the right questions but give you the framework to get the best answers for you and your company.

We believe that in almost every instance (positive or negative) there are opportunities for significant growth that will be available, albeit over small windows of time. Although early detection of such opportunities will clearly help, it's not always possible. The real option to act lies in your company's operations, information systems, and organizational culture. The ability to reconfigure and adjust these three pillars in a timely manner is the key to capitalizing on stretch opportunities. This is our main message.

Business Cases

In our book, you will find several unique stories illustrating how companies have orchestrated stretch opportunities. In each of these companies, a wide range of fleeting opportunities were generated, driven by unexpected events or unexpected market conditions. The Amazon.com story describes a significant growth opportunity in the early days of e-commerce that occurred during the Christmas peak season. The Reflect.com/P&G story talks about the challenges of mass customization and how innovative solutions leveraged the power of the rapidly emerging e-channel. The U.S. Coast Guard's story dissects their response to a natural disaster, demonstrating the power of flexible asset allocation, planning, training, and execution. The Kryptonite story describes the company's rapid recovery from a horrific event that caused a product demand collapse and widespread loss of consumer confidence in the Kryptonite brand. The regulation-driven stretch story of Watsco Inc. shows how a distributor reacted to a highly volatile period of demand during product transitions driven by environmental regulation. The United Nations Joint Logistics Center (UNJLC) story shows how a global organization improvised and adopted relief efforts in an emergency, reconfiguring available resources to meet extreme global challenges. The story of Crocs shows how the company capitalized on a fashion trend to build a company. The FreeFlow story provides alternatives to deal with inventory mismatches caused by demand shortfalls. Finally, we will discuss emerging technologies and innovative software solutions from SAP and Shipwire that allow companies to be more flexible and more agile, thus offering real options to take advantage of stretch opportunities.

A Capstone Story

Recall the story in the book *The Goal* by Eli Goldratt.[4] The book, written in the mid-1980s, continues to be used to teach operations concepts. Borrowing from the success of that book, we have created the fictitious journey of a CEO, Max Zen, and his company, Gizmo Inc. The Max Zen story is the narrative of a company that was rocked by many different events, was able to adopt and overcome unexpected challenges, and leveraged FAR to not only succeed but grow exponentially. The Gizmo story is meant to get readers thinking about their own strategies in today's volatile world.

Concept Summary

We will frame ways to capitalize on the changes of tomorrow using the FAR concept. *Agility* of a firm refers to its ability to scale rapidly to deal with volume shifts. This requires thinking in advance about how such demand shifts will be accommodated. *Flexibility* of a firm refers to how the company will accommodate product changes. This may require that all resources used in the operations are chosen to be flexible enough to accommodate shifts. This also implies that any current operational choice may not be optimal, but performance is evaluated over a longer period. Finally, *real options* refers to how choosing the right option requires consideration of external operational factors, the most cost-effective response to variability, and the ability to execute. In short, this is a book about strategic insights into how to position a firm to execute in these uncertain times, where the unexpected is quickly becoming the norm.

Wrap Up

From books to cosmetics, from helicopters to air conditioning equipment, from bicycle locks to humanitarian logistics, and from information systems to rapid logistics, these stories are a sample of the future. Let's set off on a journey to discover companies that have faced unprecedented changes and successfully defended their turf and even thrived. We promise you a thrilling ride and the ability to ask the right questions so that your organization can adapt to the new business environment.

Is This Book for You?

Imagine your business context and reflect on the time windows of projects you have been involved with this past year. Now consider how your company is organized and how you pull plans and resources and resolve to execute. Are the kinds of short-window projects that you faced synchronized with the plans of your company? If not, how should the entire company be adjusted to reflect the new realities? Is there a pattern to these short-window opportunities and how some excellent organizations have responded? What set of questions could top management focus on to prepare for such business environments? *If you are intrigued by how to answer these questions, read on. This is the book for you.*

Acknowledgments

This book has had a long gestation, with ideas and cases collected over many years of discussion, discovery, and experience. Moreover, over the years our book has benefited from feedback and thoughts from many colleagues, whose contributions we would like to gratefully acknowledge. Roger Stewart, director of Graduate Career Services at the Krannert School of Management, provided early feedback from his vantage point as a retired senior manager of the treasury for Proctor & Gamble. Ryan Menke, senior vice-president for supply chain from OFS Brands, was an early supporter of our concept. Mary Pilotte, managing director of the Global Supply Chain Management Initiative at Purdue University, provided feedback regarding the early chapters. Paul Johnston, head of business development at Watsco Inc., shared many insights into the heating, ventilating, and air-conditioning industry and provided the motivation to develop a case that morphed into the chapter in our book. Professor Svenja Sommer, from the École des Hautes Études Commerciales in Paris, was a coauthor on the case dealing with the seasonal energy efficiency ratio and environmental regulation. Professor Luk Van Wassenhove, from INSEAD, was a collaborator and researcher on humanitarian logistics and whose work and insights influenced the chapter on the United Nations Joint Logistics Committee. Several U.S. Coast Guard officers influenced the chapter on the U.S. Coast Guard's organization and capabilities. Damon Schechter, the chief executive officer for Shipwire, has an innovative supply chain vision that inspired the technology chapter. We would also like to acknowledge numerous industry experts from SAP, Proctor & Gamble, Amazon.com, FreeFlow, and many other companies we researched. Finally, to the students in executive MBA programs that have seen early versions of the cases and chapters, their feedback is gratefully acknowledged.

As always, we accept all errors and thank all our friends and colleagues for their insights. This book would not have been possible without them. Finally, our families have withstood hours of phone discussions, several rewrites, and years of promises that we would be finished—and now we finally are. We hope you, the reader, enjoy the resulting book. And if you get to orchestrate stretch opportunities with your supply chain, then we would love to hear from you.

INTRODUCTION

Orchestrating Supply Chain Opportunities

Orchestrating Supply Chain Opportunities is a concept we developed after years of collective insight into the world of strategic supply chain management. While discussing our observations in preparation for a few collaborative projects, we realized that something interesting was happening to companies worldwide—something that had yet to be quantified or collected into a single body of work. We believed that it had a powerful impact on these companies that went well beyond their strategic supply chain management; it extended into their overall competitiveness and general decision making. We began to appreciate that the many successful supply chains had one thing in common: the ability to adapt to change.

Like an orchestra, a business assembles myriad individual components and crafts order from potential chaos. Both collectives make something happen: The orchestra creates beautiful music by starting with a score and performing it for the audience, and the business fashions a product or service by designing it in the lab and selling it to the consumer. In both instances, the process leading to a finished product is more involved and complex than the finished product alone would suggest. Both, in a manner of speaking, manufacture, market, and distribute the product after organizing all the individual strands, and both choreograph, on a daily basis, the inner processes and workings of the organization so goals can be attained. Orchestration for any given business organization is the rearrangement, reconfiguring, and splicing together of various components of that organization into a cohesive design and execution for the benefit of customers, suppliers, partners, employees, and so on.

Orchestrating Supply Chain Opportunities ideally should result in taking a company's performance to a new level. Suppose a company is faced with an unforeseen chain of events that presents a significant opportunity for growth and development and, if executed correctly, will stretch the company's capabilities to such an extent that it will leave its competitors in the dust. If a company can orchestrate its capabilities to perform optimally when stretch opportunities present themselves, not only will it survive (when such survival was previously considered tenuous), but it will probably win in the market.

Just as a group of musicians must have certain coordinating protocols to allow for the seamless execution of a performance, so must the corporate entity. What is each person's capability that can be called upon at will to achieve this performance? How can the performers accomplish this unique performance? How do other unforeseen events factor in and fit seamlessly into the overall performance? How is it created? And most importantly, how is it orchestrated?

To make a musical performance a reality, several criteria have to be in play: (a) the individual musicians need some requisite level of *flexibility*, that is, the ability to play a variety of different instruments; (b) they must possess a certain degree of *agility*, that is, the ability to adjust their playing to the needs of the group as dictated by the conductor; and (c) they need to possess a tool kit of *real options*, that is, the ability to orchestrate such a performance by knowing the capabilities and boundaries of the entire ensemble. The companies described in this book all responded to the dramatic changes facing their companies by employing the criteria of flexibility, agility, and real options (FAR) in some form or another.

Business leaders across the corporate world understand that they will face potential changes, some of which might even be immediate, and that those changes will have a profound effect on the way they compete and do business. However, how other entities have dealt with similar challenges provides a guide. This book presents a compendium of real-world examples and discusses the strategies chosen, how the challenges were overcome, and how lessons learned from these examples can help corporations prepare for and overcome the changes they will face.

As long as the status quo remains intact, a business will function smoothly. But what happens when a monkey wrench is thrown into the mix, affecting an organization's ability to make music or widgets as it did in the past? The introduction of these common unplanned phenomena into a company's established, systematized way of doing business is what we term "stretch." The ability of a company to adjust to that change and how it makes that adjustment is "orchestration."

Success of the musical ensemble or corporate entity is dependent on coordination of the group's capabilities and a decision-making process—centralized, decentralized, or some combination—to attain the coordination. The unique coordination of capabilities and flexibility in the decision-making process has allowed several agencies and companies to respond successfully to opportunities. For example, when Hurricane Katrina hit in 2005, the U.S. Coast Guard orchestrated a successful response to a set of unforeseen circumstances by coordinating its varying capabilities. Rather than using a centralized command center from which all operating decisions would be made, the Coast Guard utilized a *decentralized* style in which local commanders orchestrated decisions unilaterally based on the conditions at hand and the resources available. This gave the organization a sufficient amount of agility and flexibility with respect to its assets and gave commanders real options to make things happen quickly and efficiently.

Sam Palisano, CEO of IBM, laid out the challenges faced by the modern global corporation in an influential article in *Foreign Affairs Weekly*.[1] He described a product that consisted of technology developed in the United States, a unique container developed in a lab in Sweden, a marketing message developed in London, and tracking software developed in India, with manufacturing in China, assembly in Malaysia, and labeling and distribution from a warehouse in New Jersey, and the product was sold to the U.S. consumer. In his example, what happens if demand volumes for that product increase by a significant order of magnitude? How will the supply chain orchestrate a response to this stretch in demand? What happens if a product is recalled due to a malfunction somewhere along the supply chain (i.e., an unexpected interaction between a container, the storage process in the warehouse, and the chemical inside)? How will the supply chain handle this recall efficiently? What happens when a regulatory change requires a significant product adjustment by a fixed date or when one of the sellers accuses one of the suppliers of violating intellectual property laws or corporate social responsibility norms? Or what happens if a contaminant in a chemical makes its way across the globe and is used as an ingredient by one of the suppliers throughout the supply chain? In order to survive, any given supply chain must "stretch" and respond to the aforementioned challenges, and the response orchestrated depends on the components of the supply chain.

In this book, we offer detailed real-world examples of "orchestration" and specific cases in which such "orchestration" resulted in superlative performance enabled by the supply chain. We will help you ask the right questions and make choices to enable your organization to orchestrate and meet stretch goals. Finally, we will provide a list of questions every manager should ask about his or her company in order to evaluate its current state and make the right choices to enable outstanding performance.

CHAPTER 1

Amazon.com—Orchestrating Stretch Demand

How Amazon.com Saved Christmas

During the height of the "Internet bubble," Amazon.com was one of the hottest new companies around. Jeff Bezos, Amazon's charismatic founder, had a vision that was at the core of Amazon's success: to get big, fast! He fundamentally believed that the 1990s were a unique time in history, when a new channel called the Internet would gain consumer awareness and become monetized. Bezos also believed that the window of opportunity to get a foothold in the Internet commerce space (or e-commerce, as we now call it) would be short lived. He instinctively knew that the first-mover advantage was absolutely critical to success. Moreover, his vision for Amazon, even in the early days of the company, was that it should be a *place where the consumer could discover and purchase anything online.* Yes, anything!

In order to make the dream a reality, Amazon focused on adding new products and services at an alarming rate. During this time, spending on overhead outpaced the investment in growth and the financial losses started to mount. Ironically, Amazon's stock was on the rise, but it was mostly due to the forgiving capital markets during the Internet bubble.

It is important to note that Bezos's strategy of focusing on gaining market share never blurred his ultimate vision of building a profitable business. In 1999, during the employee quarterly update, he was asked this question: "Our losses continue to mount; will we ever get to profitability?" Bezos gave a very passionate answer. He first asked, "Is there anyone in the audience who believes that I don't think profitability is important?" A short silence followed. "Please speak up, because if you do, you do not belong here."[1] There was another pause. Bezos was facing a classic CEO trade-off scenario between market share and profitability. Following a strategy focused on rapidly increasing market share required Amazon.com's supply chain to meet "stretch" growth goals and position the organization to capitalize on "stretch" opportunities.

In line with his "getting big, fast" strategy, the only parameters Bezos set concerning the variety of potential products that would be handled by the system were "we will not ship cement or gasoline." In the face of such a broad description of the company's operations and logistics strategies, Amazon's chief logistics officer, Jimmy Wright, remarked to Bezos that "if you want me to fly blind, better give me some air-space."[2] What does this mean? Design a real option in the supply chain to adapt to product and demand outcomes.

In the late 1990s, Amazon.com was in a significant hypergrowth mode. This growth forced the supply chain to scale systems, operations, and human resources rapidly. The business was growing and changing so rapidly that the physical infrastructure experienced difficulty keeping up. Most of the projects and opportunities took off faster than the company could plan for. Hence, normal goals became "stretch goals." Thus every time the company had to adapt (or stretch) to meet a goal that altered significantly from what was originally anticipated, Amazon had to redefine those goals. We consider a "stretch goal" an unplanned business opportunity necessary for a company to stay in business or required in order to take advantage of rapid growth opportunities. In particular, Amazon experienced extreme unexpected surges in demand for its products during the 1998 holiday season. If Amazon was going to survive in the emerging e-commerce realm, it would have to meet the service levels promised to consumers. Establishing lofty customer service goals was a key strategic decision, and fulfilling these goals was critical for the company's brand and success. Amazon wanted to show consumers the convenience of shopping from their homes 24-7, with next-day shipping right to their doorsteps. By executing on its customer service promise, Amazon made the bricks-and-mortar world seem sluggish, antiquated, and inconvenient to purchasers. If it appeared that Amazon could not meet the needs of the consumer and fulfill orders as promised, it would have failed. Unexpected surges in demand challenge a company to "stretch" to meet those demands; the company that can execute stretch goals efficiently will win. That is precisely what happened to Amazon.

During the 1998 holiday season, Amazon encountered an explosive surge in demand: The average December order increased 4 times from the average September order. Amazon started planning for this fourth-quarter seasonal demand increase at the beginning of the year—but not at a magnitude of 400%. Operations managers had no way of knowing how fast the business would grow. How did Amazon deal with this stretch goal to fulfill orders and meet their consumer promise?

In September of 1998, Amazon's executive management met with the senior operations management team and informed them that the peak December shipping day might reach more than 100,000 orders per day. Yes, Amazon had to adapt from approximately 25,000 orders per day to potentially more than 100,000! Needless to say, this was quite a shock to the system. The newly formed operations management team, most of whom had been with Amazon for just a few months, was in a tough spot. There was no time to scale facilities, systems, and the organization (the organization was stretched already). How did Amazon orchestrate this stretch goal efficiently?

At that time, Amazon had two distribution centers (DCs): one in Seattle, Washington, and one in Wilmington, Delaware. Both DCs ran two shifts. Both had a minimum amount of automation and mechanization. When the demand started to spike, Amazon's management had to act quickly and decisively because Amazon's brand was built on *great service*. If they could not ship orders on time, it would have been disastrous. Take the example of eToys. When eToys failed to meet its unexpected surge in demand due to the holidays and children did not receive their gifts in time for Christmas, eToys met with an untimely death. Amazon was not about to go down the tubes like eToys did.

Amazon purchased an option to have the extra buffer capacity ahead of the busy holiday shopping season—that is, an option on the flexibility and agility of its supply chain. The flexibility option involved leveraging extra physical space in the DCs that would enable Amazon to set up ad hoc processing to meet extra demand. Hence, the flexibility option gave Amazon the ability to scale physical processes and systems. The agility option required Amazon to streamline its labor force, mandating that every employee spend time working at the DCs. This gave Amazon the option to shift (scale) labor when the surge in demand occurred. The agility option enabled Amazon to leverage fulfillment space and ramp up labor quickly.

Thus Amazon has leveraged the capabilities of flexibility, agility, and real options (FAR), a paradigm that required decisive actions, and a concept we shall discuss in detail through this book. First, the operations team optimized current distribution design and space. For example, Amazon used extra DC space to set up extra pick locations for top-selling stock-keeping units (SKUs). These items were not unpacked or placed on shelves. The pallets containing these SKUs were placed in the pick locations and workers then picked items directly from the pallets. The operations team arranged additional lines for packing and shipping orders. Second, all DCs started operating in three shifts. Scaling the labor to staff all three shifts was not an easy task, but Amazon's cross-trained employees rose to the challenge. Moreover, Amazon had a wild card up its sleeve. Amazon's culture of getting the job done went beyond the employees. Not only all Amazon employees but also their families were asked to work in the DCs, picking and packing items for holiday giving. And they rose to the challenge. A staggering number of family members reported to the DCs and were quickly trained and put to work. It is important to note that every Amazon employee was an owner of the company.[3] This sense of ownership drove this incredible behavior of everyone pitching in, as required. Moreover, senior managers, including Bezos, worked the graveyard shift: from midnight to 8 a.m. This agile labor force and the use of extra space to set up additional processing lines, deployed in a very short time, allowed Amazon to succeed. Bezos always believed in not compromising on hiring great people. He was right.

Amazon orchestrated the success of its holiday performance by (a) leveraging the agility of its cross-trained employees and (b) leveraging its flexibility by expanding the physical playing field, establishing ad hoc processes, scaling through unused space, and bringing people from varied locations to increase staff capacity. The real option was their hiring of great people, a passion for performance, and a culture of execution. Moreover, what made all this possible is the actual *orchestration* by the key managers and employees, who used their experience and knowledge of Amazon's systems, processes, and highly motivated employees to get the job done. Amazon's culture of begging for forgiveness instead of asking for permission took hold and delivered.

After barely meeting the demand of the 1998 holiday season, Bezos took out an even greater option on the future by authorizing the "design and build-out of the world's most sophisticated direct-to-consumer distribution network" . . . but that's another story.

Imagine the challenges faced by supply chain managers orchestrating Amazon's operations. The fact that Amazon remains a successful e-commerce company today is a testament to their execution capability over the years. We suggest that use of FAR in supply chain choices remains a key component of Amazon's success. Consider how Amazon's lessons apply to your company. And let's move on to another context.

CHAPTER 2

The U.S. Coast Guard— Orchestrating Stretch Response

How the U.S. Coast Guard Saved Victims of Katrina

The U.S. Coast Guard (USCG) has the mission to protect the U.S. coastline and assist with major natural disasters. The performance of the Coast Guard during Hurricane Katrina was hailed as a remarkable example of execution when faced with strong negative odds. In an interview in 2010 with *Analytics* magazine, Admiral Mike Mullen, chairman of the Joint Chiefs of Staff, said that the Coast Guard "punches far above its weight class."[1] During Katrina's aftermath, the Coast Guard rescued more than 33,500 people over a few weeks—6 times as many people than the Coast Guard saved in all of 2004. As the writer in *Time* magazine put it, "So how is it that an agency that is underfunded and saddled with aging equipment—and about the size of the New York City police department—makes disaster response look like just another job, not a quagmire?"[2]

To understand how the Coast Guard executed its response, it is instructive to understand the magnitude of the "stretch" that was warranted. Hurricane Katrina was one of the largest natural disasters in U.S. history. More than 1,300 people lost their lives; several million people were displaced; and physical assets such as roads, bridges, and buildings were destroyed, generating over $200 billion in damage. When disaster struck, over 60,000 people had to be rescued from homes and rooftops, and the Coast Guard was responsible for 33,500 of those rescues. Air and boat operations by the Coast Guard lasted 17 days. Barely 3 days into the response, 43 aircraft and 2,000 USCG personnel were on site.[3]

People were hoisted amid downed power lines, flying debris, and other obstacles that are not commonly present during typical USCG search-and-rescue missions. More than 8 million gallons of fuel spilled and had to be cleaned up. This required working with local and federal authorities to create a maritime environmental response.

To accomplish all of these tasks, helicopters were needed. In anticipation of the storm, helicopters moved out of Mobile, Alabama, and New Orleans. As soon as the storm passed, helicopters flew in from those bases and from all 26 air stations throughout the country. Each air station prioritized its tasks and dropped the less serious tasks in order to maintain readiness. The crews combined to form rescue teams independent of their origins. Even as far away as Cape Cod, commanders got ready to move assets to assist. The entire surge was accommodated within days. When the tasks were completed, the aircraft and crew returned to their air stations and resumed normal operations.

At the end of the operation, the USCG evaluated its response and created a set of lessons learned from its performance. The cost of this operation had to be tabulated and recovered from the Federal Emergency Management Agency (FEMA) and other sources. The bill, reported to be less than $20 million, certainly classifies as an efficient response. When it was all over, unlike most other agencies, the performance of the USCG was characterized as outstanding in all federal performance reviews. But what aspects of the supply chain permitted them to gracefully accommodate the tremendous surge in demand?

The General Accounting Office (GAO) identified as key to the Coast Guard's exceptional performance its cross-training, standardization of equipment and task routines, centralized information visibility across assets, and the ability to quickly prioritize and release assets to their most required locations.[4] It is clear that such a heroic performance does not happen without planning or without a clear sense of operational performance being considered at the highest level of the organization. But notice that the investments in cross-training, standardization, information visibility are actually "real options"—they enable harnessing of capacity when events unfold. These investments permit teams drawn from different bases to come together quickly, thus permitting flexibility of deployment. Finally, centralized information visibility permits task prioritization and pooling of assets and thus affords agility. Clearly, flexibility, agility, and real options (FAR) is a readily recognizable concept at work within the Coast Guard's system.

Discussions with USCG personnel suggest that while Katrina created severe stretch at the USCG for a short period, it was accommodated by adjusting the rest of the system so that at the end of the year there was a minimal lingering effect on the assets that were used. In other words, accommodating stretch required a careful assessment of priorities and the ranking of tasks that could be postponed, delegated to others, or cancelled altogether. This ability to stretch to accommodate a significant event but return back to normalcy as soon as the event passes is a unique capability and strategy.

As described in several contexts, a hallmark of the USCG is a decentralized organization that allows for decision-making autonomy and flexibility. On the Gulf Coast, this autonomy and flexibility mattered well before Katrina hit. On August 27, 2005, the day before the mayor of New Orleans ordered a mandatory evacuation, the Coast Guard began moving its personnel out of the region. Officers left helicopters and boats in a ring around the area so that they could move in behind the storm, no matter which direction it took. "We have extraordinary autonomy to move assets," explained USCG admiral Thad Allen during a flyover of the Mississippi Gulf Coast region a few weeks after Katrina. "I don't think any other agency has the ability to do that."[5] The Coast Guard was also able to call on auxiliaries who had been involved in planning and preparation and thus provided surge capacity. Finally, it was expected that leadership would move to the particular individual with the expertise, regardless of rank.

To continue operations in the absence of communications links, USCG personnel relied on plans that had been exercised and that did not require detailed data. In addition, prestaged communication equipment and predistributed satellite and cell phones all enabled operations to continue with minimal coordination.

There are a few key USCG principles that permit such execution. The principle of flexibility in the USCG system requires that multiple possible missions be executed using the same people and assets by adjusting to the tasks and situations. This is crucial for the USCG because its responsibilities evolve over time: from search and rescue, to homeland security, to assistance in catastrophes. Such responsibilities demand the ability to conduct "surge operations"—high-intensity efforts at short notice in response to emergencies. Such surge operations require coordination across personnel and assets by adapting to locate resources while continuing regular operations. The feasibility of such plans depends on the standardization of processes, assets, training, and so on so that units can be composed of personnel from any air station, pulled together at short notice, and still function effectively as a team. In short, flexibility is a key component of the USCG's ability to respond to stretch requirements.

Another important strength of the USCG system is the latitude provided to personnel to act quickly without waiting for specific direction. An example provided in the GAO report describes the initiative taken by a junior pilot of a C-130 aircraft, who, on arriving in New Orleans, recognized the dire need for a communications platform. She changed her mission from environmental inspection to setting up an airborne communication platform. This initiative, done based on her judgment, provided critical information that enabled improved performance across all assets.

The USCG, as a matter of course, does advanced planning and training for potential stretch requirements. At the onset of a mission, senior commanders are obligated to develop a plan for personnel and assets that can credibly execute the stretch requirements. This may include rescheduling, prioritizing or eliminating existing tasks, requesting resources from other units, coordinating with local resources, and so on. In short, flexibility, agility, and access to shared resources (i.e., real options), as well as the use of a combination of centralized and decentralized issuance of commands on the scene, allow them to provide the surge capability that is characteristic of the Coast Guard's excellence. Finally, lessons learned after each such operation are documented, which allows for the codification of processes that worked, identification of gaps, and planning of training-related changes to improve performance for the next event. Such reflection is a key step in developing efficient stretch.

The USCG's performance during Hurricane Katrina shows a significant "stretch" capability of the supply chain. What can be learned by private corporations from an understanding of their performance? We focus on such issues in later chapters.

Excellent Private-Sector Examples

But beside the USCG, there were other corporations that excelled. An issue of *Fortune* magazine celebrated private companies that thrived amid the challenges posed by Hurricane Katrina.[6] One such company was Wal-Mart. Managers of Wal-Mart stores in Katrina's path focused on opening the stores as soon as possible and providing all the products they could—at no cost for a period of time—to enable the local population to get food and water quickly. Food, water, medicine, flashlights, and temporary cooking equipment were all brought in as soon as possible, all coordinated by an emergency team that was brought into service as soon as the hurricane made its appearance. As an article in the *Washington Post* describes, Wal-Mart had trucks filled with goods ready to deploy even before the hurricane reached land. Employees who relocated were permitted to take jobs in other stores throughout the country. The *Washington Post* reports,

> During a tearful interview on *Meet the Press*, Aaron F. Broussard, president of Jefferson Parish in the New Orleans suburbs, told host Tim Russert that if "the American government would have responded like Wal-Mart has responded, we wouldn't be in this crisis."[7]

The article goes on to say that

> "preparations at the Brookhaven distribution center ensured that goods desperately needed by ravaged sections of the Gulf Coast started appearing on Wal-Mart shelves." It helped that Wal-Mart in 2004 had set a policy of price freezes during hurricanes, according to Professor Steven Horwitz, who has studied the company's response extensively.[8]

It also helped that Wal-Mart stores provide considerable flexibility at the local level for managers to act decisively. Descriptions of independent local action abounded. Horwitz describes managers who distributed much-needed free medicine. They broke down distribution center walls to get access to products. They permitted people to sleep in stores. They permitted anyone to use their company intranet to post messages and pictures. In short, the company leveraged the flexibility to move people, the agility to run its distribution center to ramp up quickly, and the real option to build up supplies in anticipation of demand. FAR worked for Wal-Mart, with management's strategic choices enabling its execution. The then CEO of

Wal-Mart said, "A lot of you are going to have to make decisions above your level. Make the best decision that you can with the information that's available to you at the time, and, above all, do the right thing."[9]

On its website,[10] the company summarized its efforts:

- "2,450 Wal-Mart truck loads have been dispatched to communities throughout the Gulf States and Texas, including 100 truckloads of donated merchandise."
- "Wal-Mart has provided its drivers and trucks in special instances to acquire and transport relief supplies, water, food and clothing donated by outside community members and organizations wanting to assist residents of Louisiana and Mississippi."
- "Through Wal-Mart Photo Centers and Walmart.com, pictures of friends and loved ones can be posted on-line for free at any store to assist in efforts to locate and find those who could be missing."
- "Wal-Mart nationwide announced it would fill prescriptions, free of charge, to evacuees with emergency medicine needs and no money, even if they did not have a copy of their prescription."
- "Wal-Mart offered free check cashing in approximately 126 stores in the hurricane disaster area for an initial two-week period. This included government, payroll and insurance checks and computer-generated checks."
- "[Wal-Mart] donated the use of 25 vacant facilities in impacted states for relief efforts. Uses include evacuee shelters, supply depots, food pantry, and a tent city for utility crews and even a dialysis clinic. The company will pay utilities on these facilities while in use."

Clearly, all of these efforts had to involve improvisation, but they required the support of a superb supply chain that could rise to the occasion. We submit that creating such capabilities requires senior management commitment and specific actions. FAR came through for Wal-Mart, just as it did for the U.S. Coast Guard. We believe much can be learned from these organizations. We also believe that learning can be encapsulated in the concept of FAR customized to the problem at hand.

CHAPTER 3

Reflect.com—Orchestrating Stretch Innovation

How Procter & Gamble Leveraged Innovation on the Internet

Reflect.com was Procter & Gamble's (P&G's) failed Internet start-up. We decided to include the story of Reflect.com for one simple reason: One often learns more from failure than from success. And while Reflect.com failed as a business, the lessons learned may well live on in P&G's products and supply chain choices.

In the late 1990s, P&G was toying with the revolutionary concept of creating a custom beauty brand for the masses. The underlying premise was that if we assume every woman is unique, then her beauty care products should reflect *her* uniqueness and individuality. The vision was grand: to create custom beauty products (from skin care, to shampoo, to cosmetics, to fine fragrance), one at a time, for *each woman* . . . a unique, customized product that would even have her name on it.

Pioneering a mass-customized beauty brand, in which the products do not exist until the consumer creates them, was unequivocally charting new territory. This revolutionary concept was forged in P&G's beauty care division under the leadership of A. G. Lafley, who was the division president at the time but went on to become the chairman and the CEO of P&G. In P&G's disciplined and rigorous style, the company began testing this revolutionary concept with consumers under the project code name "Mirror." To begin with, a small, dedicated team of research and development (R&D) and marketing professionals was assembled, a modest budget was set aside, and the research began. The first step was to test the "custom beauty" concept with consumers. The results were extremely favorable. In fact, the concept scored very high—much higher than anticipated. It was clear that consumers truly liked the idea of a "custom beauty" brand: a perfect color, shade, scent, or active ingredient that reflects the consumer—that is uniquely *hers*.

The incubation of and research for this unique concept took place just as the Internet revolution was sweeping across America. Amazon .com was an aggressive start-up, but new and innovative ideas were popping up all over the Internet, and a new lexicon was born—e-business, e-commerce, e-channels, e-enterprises. The brains at P&G were intrigued by this new channel and wanted to participate in its growth and success. P&G is renowned for innovation, and piloting a mass-customized beauty brand delivered through the new e-commerce channel is about as innovative as it gets.

Orchestrating such a vision, particularly within the world's largest consumer goods company, was, to say the least, a challenge. The only efficient way to drive this type of cutting-edge innovation was to do something different, something that wasn't normally done within P&G. P&G's senior executives immediately recognized that it would not be possible to develop such a business inside the traditional halls of P&G. This may seem trivial to the outsider, but the culture inside P&G is admittedly and very deliberately homogeneous, with a meticulous hiring process and a lifetime practice of cultivating internal employee development. Promotions are driven strictly from within, and everything is systematized, standardized, and organized. Thus the decision was made to spin out this business, create a limited liability company (LLC), and call it Reflect.com.

P&G pushed the "out-of-the-box" envelope even further and partnered with a blue-chip venture capital firm in the Silicon Valley: Redpoint Ventures. Redpoint knew how to develop and manage a start-up. The decision was then made to locate the company in San Francisco, where one would find an abundance of experienced and talented employees uniquely suited to build an Internet business. In order to understand "stretch innovation" and all it implies, it is necessary to clarify some of the challenges P&G had to overcome.

1. *Building a mass-customized product supply chain.* Clearly, using a conventional manufacturing, supply chain, and distribution model was not an option to produce small-volume, mass-customized

beauty products. It just was not scalable. To manufacture one product at a time for each of the women in America would require a warehouse the size of New Jersey. Indeed, when interviewing Reflect's future chief logistics officer, P&G's chief financial officer (CFO) Clayton Daily (a Reflect.com board member) said, "The business model presumes we can make a wide breadth of products, one at a time. We don't have anyone at P&G with this expertise. Do you know how to solve this problem?" The interviewee replied, "No, I do not, and frankly I don't believe anyone does . . . but I would be willing to try and figure it out."[1] Simply put, the supply chain necessary to operate this business had never been built before in the beauty care industry. It is clear that flexibility was essential, but remember that overall volumes were still unknown. Thus agility was a key capability, too.

2. *Researching and developing.* Developing thousands of unique products or stock-keeping units (SKUs) requires complex science and a hefty investment in R&D. This is not like mixing paint at a hardware store. Customers would be using these products on their faces and hair, so the formulations had to be tested for safety, stability, microcontamination, and so on. How could Reflect guarantee products would perform well and, most importantly, be safe? Normally, P&G required years of testing to perfect a single formulation. How could it test products as they were being developed for consumers? Reflect had to figure out how to test the customized products but bring the products to the customer quickly and safely. This was a huge challenge. Product design was thus key; a modular product design would enable combinations of ingredients, each with their own key benefits, to be assembled to build the final product.

3. *Manufacturing.* Imagine a normal P&G manufacturing plant and run-of-the-mill production line running during an 8-hour shift producing more than 10,000 units per day: efficient, high speed, and optimized for maximum throughput like a Swiss watch. But the requirements from Reflect were different: to produce one unit at a time . . . at a reasonable cost . . . and quickly. With modular designs, Reflect.com's supply chain had the flexibility to make or buy individual components and assemble them on demand.

4. *Naming your own product.* As part of the customization experience, P&G wanted consumers to name each product: Sally's 2-in-1 Shampoo, Melanie's Eye Gel, and Marcia's Radiant Lipstick. Why? Because the brand is all about *the consumer* and should *reflect* each woman's individual beauty. Naming *your* products significantly helps to create this brand equity; each woman becomes fully vested in the products she creates. It sounds simple, but technologically the hurdles were colossal. For example, labels had to be printed for each product after it was created and purchased by a consumer. Thus labeling had to occur at the distribution center rather than at the production plant. If the customer wanted her name etched on the bottle, then that needed to happen, too. And all this had to happen quickly and accurately for each customer.

5. *Determining which products are right for a particular person.* Just because a product is made one at a time, just for *me*, is it really the best product for *me*? The profiling process would have to be developed online—there is no cosmetics counter or beauty salon to visit, and the customer cannot physically smell the product, feel its texture, or see what colors look best. Therefore, a process had to be developed and perfected to solve this complex issue. Again, this is not an easy task. Here, the website user experience was the key: It had to have an interactive and engaging user interface that permitted an experience equivalent to the beauty care salesperson, but it had to be virtual and thus more efficient. For example, consumers were taken through a unique user experience, on-line, consisting of specific questions and visual cues. Behind the scenes, product development and IT experts were able map consumer input to a complex decision trees algorithm, profiling each consumer into "her" perfect product.

To orchestrate this complex web of variables, Reflect.com managers had to innovate and solve difficult problems. Reflect's organization had to be fluid in structure and reactive to change, and the supply chain had to be built with a high degree of flexibility. Reflect's product development and website had to possess high levels of agility for the business to become viable. This fluid, flexible, and agile company managed incredible breakthroughs during its 5-year life. All this time, customer delight was nurtured. In the early years, when a woman ordered from Reflect, she was sent a live orchid via Federal Express just to say thank you. Such customer pampering had to be accompanied by order accuracy and product quality, along with on-time delivery, to be credible.

The team at Reflect relied on ingenuity and innovation to overcome these challenges. Reflect developed a modular manufacturing technique that allowed for rapid line setup and quick product changeovers to produce just a few units at a time during each production run. The entire line was modular . . . on wheels! Everything was moving all the time. When one component was being sanitized, another was being staged and yet another was being removed and swapped out. Standard assembly and packing equipment was modified in numerous ways to accommodate this constant flow. Flexibility was the common denominator for everything they did. Reflect achieved 29 line changes in a single 7.5 hour shift. Furthermore, Reflect decided to modularize production outside the manufacturing plant and complete the manufacturing process at the distribution facility. This meant Reflect could produce modular components at the plant and then assemble finished goods at the distribution center. Imagine the possibilities. Finally, Reflect piloted a custom beauty experience, not just on-line, but also in retail. Reflect opened beauty counters in Marshal Fields department stores. To deliver custom products in retail, the company managed to push the final product assembly to the retail counter, right in the department store. When a consumer arrived at the counter, she was able to select her base formula, her active ingredient, her fragrance, and even name and design the label of her moisturizer right at the beauty counter.

No one could have thought this possible, but it happened. We interpret Reflect's supply chain design as following the idea of flexibility, agility, and real options (FAR). Flexibility within the supply chain, agility within product development, and fluidity within the organization produced real options for management to innovate, make difficult choices, learn, and overcome challenges. This is a textbook-perfect example of stretch innovation, and that is why, despite its failure, it is included in this book.

So what happened to Reflect.com? Why was it not successful? The simple answer is that consumer adoption for Reflect customized products was not strong enough to sustain the company. P&G brought the lessons and intellectual property (IP) back to the "mother ship" and closed

Reflect's operations in San Francisco. Today, the variety in any given line of P&G beauty care and personal care products is richer than in the past. Where there used to be two Head & Shoulders products, now there is a formulation for any conceivable combination of attributes: dry scalp, colored hair, sensitive scalp, oily hair, oily scalp, and so on. A coincidence? Or lessons learned from Reflect and leveraged into P&G's billion-dollar brands? You make the call.

CHAPTER 4

Watsco—Orchestrating Stretch Opportunities

How Watsco Navigated a Perfect Storm

Did you know that the U.S. Department of Energy (DOE) plans to make new U.S. residential customers net-zero energy users by 2020 and commercial buildings net-zero energy consumers by 2025? Imagine houses with solar panels on the roof; quiet 17 Seasonal Energy Efficiency Ratio (SEER) heat pump water heaters; airtight, moisture-managed construction of structural insulated panels; and an integrated design that allows most of the home's plumbing to reside within one wall, saving precious energy. Finally, consider the credit for electricity piped back into the grid. Now imagine how all of these changes will be accomplished across products and customers. How will we get from the present to this vision of the future?

Accomplishing these changes will require a combination of incentive carrots and regulatory sticks, all of which will impact the corresponding industry supply chains. Anticipate turmoil or opportunity, depending on whether you view a glass as half-full or half-empty. Every industry participant will potentially strive to maximize his or her profit during the transition as customers choose their responses to product transitions. Going green is bound to generate upheaval as the country balances desired change with the practical cost of altering existing capabilities and distributing associated expenses.

A great example of such a regulation-driven perfect storm occurred in 2006 in the home air-conditioning industry. By the time the dust settled, the entire supply chain had gone through a rough transition, with winners and losers at all stages of the supply chain. We describe details here but suggest that you, the reader, visualize if your industry is a candidate for such a perfect storm. If so, consider how the management of your supply chain could enable you to participate in the upside of such transitions. But before we delve into such details, here is some background regarding the industry and its rocky transition.

An article published in the *Miami Herald* in June 2006 describes a significant improvement in the fortunes of Watsco, the nation's largest heating and cooling distributor:

> Coconut Grove-based Watsco's business is hot. Watsco—the largest distributor of air-conditioning, heating and refrigeration products in the United States—is benefiting from new federal guidelines that require air conditioners to be more energy efficient, which usually means they're also more expensive.
>
> Other factors are helping the company too: Home construction is up this year, thanks to interest rates that are still relatively low. And it doesn't hurt that central air conditioners have a "useful life" of 15 years.
>
> Last year, Watsco's revenue jumped roughly 28 percent to $1.682 billion. Net income increased 45 percent to $70 million.[1]

The history of regulatory changes in the air-conditioning industry makes for interesting drama. The genesis for this story takes place on January 22, 2001: the last day of President Clinton's administration. The DOE issued a 13 SEER rule, which increased energy efficiency requirements of home air-conditioning systems by 30% compared to the earlier 10 SEER minimum standard. The SEER is a measure of cooling efficiency defined as the total cooling output (in British thermal units, or BTUs) provided by a unit during its normal annual usage divided by the total energy input (in watt hours) during the same period. This minimum SEER rule was expected to produce a significant change in the market because more than 75% of the equipment sold was rated at the minimum efficiency. Such products compete mainly on price and share similar features.

Industry groups opposed this standard as soon as the change was announced. The primary reasons were that equipment sizes would increase (almost double), equipment costs (for a typical home) would increase by about 30%, and the associated tools and so on used for installation would have to change, thus also increasing costs. As a result, initial out-of-pocket expenses for homeowners would increase as would space requirements for the new equipment. Manufacturing plants would have to undergo significant modifications to accommodate these new requirements. Adding to the complexity of the situation, the technology used to attain the 13 SEER was also in a state of flux (more on that later). In short, there were (and are) significant choices for alternate technologies, including variable-speed motor controls and advanced compressor and microchannel heat exchanger technology choices.

Under the new presidential administration of George W. Bush, the DOE delayed the effective date for implementation to April 23, 2001. On March 23, 2001, the American Refrigeration Institute (ARI) filed a petition for reconsideration and urged the DOE to relax the standard to a 12 SEER. A change to the 12 SEER would minimize the disruption to the supply chain and also improve efficiency by 20% over the then-current minimum 10 SEER standard.

However, the DOE estimated that between 2006 and 2030, a 13 SEER standard would save the equivalent of the annual energy consumption of 26 million households and result in a net savings of $1 billion to consumers by 2020. By choosing a 13 SEER instead of a 12 SEER standard, the construction of 12 power plants (in total 400 mega-watts) would be avoided, reducing nitrous-oxide emissions by 12,000 metric tons and cutting greenhouse gas emissions by 9 million metric tons of carbon. Finally, the DOE claimed that the improved air-conditioning would help when air quality is poor, that is, on hot days. On April 20, 2001, the DOE issued a postponement and reconsideration with an intention to relax the standard to a 12 SEER. A consumer lawsuit was filed by several states (Maine, New Jersey, Nevada, Vermont, Connecticut, New York, and California) and by consumer groups such as the Natural Resources Defense Council and the Consumer Federation of America against the secretary of the DOE and the DOE, ARI, Texas Ratepayers Organization, Massachusetts, and Rhode Island. The lawsuit claimed that the DOE had not followed proper procedures in its rollback and requested that the 13 SEER standard be reinstated. On January 13, 2004, the U.S. Court of Appeals for the Second Circuit ruled that indeed the DOE had not followed proper procedures and required that the 13 SEER be reinstated.

Thus the DOE requirement that all equipment manufactured after January 23, 2006, should be a minimum of 13 SEER would be enforced per the schedule. However, contractors could continue to purchase and install 10 SEER air-conditioning units, provided they were manufactured before January 23, 2006. Thus manufacturers, distributors, and contractors could sell their 10 SEER inventory long after the manufacturing cutoff date. However, buying the equipment is one thing; individual counties and states would decide if occupancy permits would be issued for residences with equipment with less than 13 SEER ratings.

The new 13 SEER air-conditioning units would be larger, thus only 171 of these units could be packed into a trailer versus 325 of the 10 SEER units. The material costs for the 13 SEER would be larger because most of the efficiency would come from added surface area for the condensing coils. Dealer warehouses would have to grow larger to maintain current inventory levels. Manufacturers would see higher labor costs to handle the units. The systems would also use about 40% more refrigerant than 10 SEER models.

In addition, the United States ratified the Montreal Protocol on Substances That Deplete the Ozone Layer in 1998 and passed the Clean Air Act in 1990. The Environmental Protection Agency (EPA) thus planned a phaseout of hydrochlorofluorocarbon (HCFC). As of 2010, no new equipment can use R-22 (an HCFC). By 2020, all production of R-22 will cease. To plan for this phaseout, the EPA announced rules in January 2003 that stopped most imports from Asia and eastern Europe. As a result of plant closings and fewer competing manufacturers, prices were expected to be up to 70% higher than in 2001. Historical data regarding the phaseout of R-12 between 1990 and 2000 showed the price increased from $80 per 30 lbs to more than $800 toward the end of the phaseout. This suggested that 13 SEER air-conditioning units using R-22 would face similar phaseout-related refrigerant price increases but would face a greater effect because they used a higher quantity (40% more).

This means that alternative refrigerants will need to be considered for the future. One choice is 407C, a blend of hydrofluorocarbons (HFCs) whose physical properties and operating performance permit them to be used as a direct substitute for R-22. However, 407C lowers the performance of unmodified R-22 units by 5%–10% and will make the units more costly for the same SEER than R-22 based units. It will thus increase the costs to attain the 13 SEER. An alternative is 410A, a mixture of another set of HFCs. It operates at a substantially higher pressure (50%–70% higher) than R-22 and cannot be dropped into an existing R-22 unit. But the modified system may be able to achieve the same performance of an R-22 at a slightly lower cost. The higher pressure warrants smaller tube diameters or thicker tube walls, which will increase costs for manufacturers as they convert plants to handle the smaller tube diameters and stricter contamination standards. It is thus unclear how much the 2010 rule changes will affect manufacturers' 13 SEER product offerings.

Some manufacturers announced significant capital investments and significant design changes, while others stuck to designs that were less efficient but easier to transition. Distributors used up significant working capital reserves to build up 10 SEER inventory. When manufacturers started sourcing their new designs, many ended up using similar components, thus creating supply shortages. These valve manufacturers in turn rushed to build up capacity, thus creating machine-tool bottlenecks.

Utility companies in Texas started offering special incentives for customers to trade up to even more efficient models (14 SEER and higher). The new 13 SEER models used a lot more copper tubing, but copper prices started increasing significantly as world copper demand increased. Housing starts in the United States faced volatility. Some manufacturers could not manage their product launches effectively, thus creating 13 SEER supply shortages. Data collected and published monthly by ARI had historically provided manufacturer and distributor shipments and inventories. These data showed significant volatility, finally resulting in ARI dropping some of the data collection and reporting due to significant forecast errors.

Understanding Supply Chain Issues

The air-conditioning regulatory transition is a classic situation with stretch opportunities for a successfully managed supply chain. Recognizing the potential turmoil from the introduction of new products, some distributors stocked up on 10 SEER units in advance of the January 22, 2006, deadline. This served as a hedge against disruptions anticipated from the new product launch and provided the industry with a real option.

But to choose the right level, some distributors centralized control of inventories nationwide, thus providing the ability to quickly respond to new products, regional permit variation, and customer preference revelations. For example, data collected in 2006 showed an unusual phenomenon: customers shifted to more expensive 14 SEER and 15 SEER units that were already 2010 compliant. Flexibility in providing the desired customer variant required careful control of the stock-keeping units (SKUs) that would be offered in each region and pricing to ride the corresponding demand wave that ensued.

Finally, there were often regional demand surges for specific SKUs as manufacturers outlined their strategies and associated pricing. The industry consisted of a patchwork of independent and company-owned distributor networks, all competing to satisfy customer demand. Close coordination with manufacturers permitted distributors to understand how plans unfolded, anticipate supplier bottlenecks, and so on. This allowed distributors to have a better sense of demand evolution than that indicated by ARI data. The associated agility enabled select distributors to benefit from the market volatility.

In short, supply chain participants who possessed the requisite attributes of flexibility, agility, and real options (FAR) and could thus harness the upside succeeded. The same happened at the manufacturer end. While some manufacturers like Carrier announced a significant earnings impact due to slow product ramp-up and manufacturing issues, others had a great launch—albeit with simpler designs that had built-in real option choices that could maneuver through commodity price shifts, valve availability, and so on. All of this suggests that supply chain structure and thus the ability to orchestrate stretch requires some carefully considered choices that can accommodate the agility and flexibility demanded in such product transitions.

Many such regulated product changes can be expected to impact the industry as the federal government continues to impose energy efficiency requirements on society. Imagine the choices manufacturers will have to make as they choose how to ramp down the volumes of the old products to phase in the new ones. How significant should design changes be while accommodating existing legacy capacity? How will installation and repair systems be structured to service old and new models? How will customers react—will they rush to install old equipment, delay installation of new equipment until teething problems and learning curves are realized, or move to more efficient models as the price premium for this additional efficiency decreases? These questions are relevant for the entire firm, across its functional areas, as working capital pressures, capacity expansion, marketing challenges, and competitive choices all face a perfect storm.

There will be winners and losers, as the air-conditioning equipment industry shows, but perhaps the most important question is what can be done to manage manufacturing through such turmoil. The demonstrated financial performance of Watsco suggests that their ability to manage in a volatile yet high-upside environment suggests that it can be done.

Capitalizing on supply chain stretch opportunities in such contexts requires companies to rapidly synchronize supply with customer demand as consumers reveal their proclivity for energy efficiency changes, as the impact of the regulation on product attribute choices becomes apparent (e.g., whether the Kyoto 2010 requirement is demanded in older products), and as the replacement market either stalls and waits for new product offerings or accelerates and uses the old products available in inventory. Imagine what it takes to orchestrate supply chain stretch in such situations.

CHAPTER 5

Kryptonite Lock Company— Orchestrating Survival

How the Blogs Unlocked the Secret of Kryptonite

The Kryptonite lock is a brand of bicycle lock that secures a bicycle when the owner leaves it in a public place. Kryptonite's parent company, Ingersoll-Rand, claims that Kryptonite represents 1% of the company's $10 billion in sales. The lock was developed in 1972 by Chicago Lock. The lock, named after the material that can defeat Superman, promised invincibility.

The design consisted of a U-shaped piece made of hardened steel with a circular cross-section and a removable crossbar. A pin tumbler locking mechanism was the main component of the lock. The bicycle can thus be secured to a pole using this lock. The company used independent third-party testing agencies to test the security of their locks. Kryptonite's New York line, the Fahgettaboudit lock, carried a $3,500 replacement warranty in the event of the theft of the bicycle. The company claimed that the locks were resistant to "bolt cutters, saws, hammers and chisels."[1]

In 1992, a British bicycling magazine published an article by journalist John Stuart Clark describing the weaknesses of the tubular pin tumbler mechanism by picking a lock using a ballpoint pen.[2] Though the story was covered by some television stations in Europe, it did not receive wide publicity. Blogs continued to talk about it for a while. The articles did not mention the Kryptonite lock but focused on security and the fact that determined thieves can break into anything. The Kryptonite Lock Company has since been sold and bought since then, with little company memory of that initial article and the potential vulnerability of the Kryptonite lock.

In 2004, Chris Brennan of San Francisco described opening an expensive Kryptonite bicycle lock using a Bic pen with four slits in the end of the pen's barrel to ease it in and open the lock with a single twist.

The story was tested by *Wired* magazine, which managed to open the Kryptonite Evolution 2000 lock in seconds using the procedure.[3] A YouTube video showed customers that if someone were to insert the back of a plastic Bic pen into the circular barrel of the lock and turn it, then the lock would open. Chicago attorney Mike Tobias also publicized the flaw by showing that laptop security locks that also use an axial pin tumbler design could be opened with a pen or a toilet-paper tube.

Finally, on September 17, 2004, the *New York Times* printed an article titled "A Ballpoint Trick Infuriates Bicyclists."[4] The article described the YouTube video and associated news and described how to pick the Kryptonite U-lock. This was identified as a concern for any product that used a tubular cylinder as part of the locking mechanism, including bicycle locks and locks on vending machines, coin-operated machines, and other security products. Other readers checked and confirmed that their gun-cabinet locks could also be picked using a Bic pen.

Bicycle owners tested this vulnerability using their own Bic pens and were stunned to discover that they could easily pick their locks. The problem affected the company's Evolution lock, KryptoLok lock, New York chain, New York Noose chain, Evolution Disc lock, Kryptodisc lock, and DFS Disc lock. In the past, bicycle shops had overwhelmingly recommended these locks to bike owners. As news spread, bicycle shops pulled the locks from their shelves and cyclists started leaving their bikes at home. While the same design was used by millions of locks, the focus remained on Kryptonite, which had the largest market share. Bicycle shops recommended that owners replace the Kryptonite with a sturdy $20 (at most) padlock available at hardware stores.

That's when the volume of bloggers started exploding and the Internet buzz took off. The number of blog readers grew from almost zero on September 12, to 1.8 million on September 19 of that year, and the company announced a free product exchange on September 22, with an estimated cost of $10 million. A figure in a 2005 issue of *Fortune* magazine shows the data graphically.[5]

Kryptonite managers discuss the fact that in the blogosphere, information moves in nanoseconds. Bloggers and forum posters are not required to check their stories. Competitors can sign on and attack a company's brand. And while this groundswell of attacks on a product occurs in virtual space, the logistics of a response in the real world can appear to be at a snail's pace. This is because supply chain orchestration requires planning, production capacity, materials, transportation, contracts, and risk-sharing agreements—all of which are the bane of business transactions in the real world. Orchestrating supply requires time—something that creates a mismatch between preferred response time and actual response time.

Bloggers in turn suggest that this shows the need for companies to monitor blogs and thus get an early read of upcoming events. The Kryptonite Lock Company received *Business 2.0* magazine's Dumbest Moments in Business 2004 award for its handling of the issue. The *Fortune* article suggests that freewheeling bloggers can boost a product or destroy it—this being an example of destruction.[6]

The event could not have come at a worse time. The company was getting ready to launch at the Eurobike and Interbike shows. Manufacturing had been switched on and was ramping up. The company decided not to respond to bloggers but to focus on releasing their message on the company website. Ingersoll-Rand assisted with crisis planning and customer service. The phone system went into overload, and the company website recorded significant hits.

For the first week, the company remained quiet, only releasing a statement that their locks remained a deterrent. During that time, they worked on getting a better lock ready for release. The company then responded by working quickly to get a different mechanism to bicycle shops that used a disc-based design. All owners were promised a program to upgrade their locks to new ones. This upgrade was available for all existing locks, including those purchased over 10 years ago. This upgrade program was available to all distributors internationally so as not to disadvantage any dealer, distributor, or consumer, regardless of location. The company promised to replace 100,000 Bic-pickable designs.

There continued to be problems associated with handling the returned locks, dealing with profit erosion all through 2005, and reassuring the distribution channels that the new locks would work effectively. Competitors quietly worked to improve their designs and release to the market.

But soon there was another attack on the redesigned U-lock in a bike forum.[7] This time around, the company responded aggressively. The report suggested that an "ordinary wire cutter" could be used to break into the Kryptonite lock. However, Kryptonite's public relations director, Donna Tucci, pointed out immediately that the wire cutters cost between $600 and $700 and were tools that were not used by ordinary thieves. The blog apparently originated from a competitor, who used this attempt to slam Kryptonite's new claims. The company claimed that the New York Fahgettaboudit lock, which was covered by the antitheft protection offer, had no claims of property being stolen. In the end, the immediate response and the aggressive stance by the company thwarted the competitor's attempt and was recognized as an effective response to a blogger's attack.

It is clear that Kryptonite faced a serious attack that originated in the blogosphere, migrated to traditional newspaper media, and overwhelmed the company with its simplicity. While the bits of news traveled at the speed of light, the response in physical space required the orchestration of suppliers, manufacturers, transporters, distributors, and customers as well as those handling returns. This physical space thus had to be planned to anticipate such possible threats. But how can the supply chain be adjusted to deal with such downsides? It is clear that such downsides, if not handled effectively, can easily morph into strategic threats to the company as a whole.

But in the end, Kryptonite's orchestration of its supply chain response through immediate design changes, coordination with suppliers and distributors, and a willingness to replace all inventory for retailers and customers served as a remarkable story of success. Note the connections to the flexibility, agility, and real options (FAR) concept. The blog-generated noise died down, and the company continued to retain its customers.

However, not all blog threats are negative. An example of a significant positive swarm caused by blogger advice is the Voltaic backpack: a backpack designed with built-in solar panels to enable hikers to keep their gadgets charged. The product was mentioned on the Cool Hunting blog, moved on to Gizmodo, and so on. The impact was a flurry of orders that forced a planned launch to become a scramble to handle orders. Another example is the jump in interest iLike, the website designed by twin brothers Ali and Hadi Partovi. The site was inaugurated on May 25, 2007, at 1 a.m., saw 10,000 users by 3 p.m., saw another 30,000 in the next 5 hours, and, in the next few weeks, grew to 1 million and then 6 million users. The breakneck growth emanated from the viral growth facilitated by the Facebook plug-in they offered to share musical preferences. The physical world demanded a rapid increase in server capacity, programming to handle this significant workload, and then a rush of venture capitalists to fund this growth. The blog and virtual world had pushed the physical world to cater to its whims.

CHAPTER 6

The United Nations Joint Logistics Center— Orchestrating Humanitarian Logistics

How the UNJLC Coordinates Relief for Victims of Global Catastrophes

During complex emergencies, challenges evolve in a fast and unpredictable manner. When humanitarian emergencies arise, responses have to be coordinated between unfamiliar partners: military forces, local authorities, and nongovernmental organizations (NGOs). Given a shortage of logistics assets, successful execution requires having the ability to prioritize tasks, allocate responsibilities across possible providers, develop consensus across providers, deploy personnel, attract donor funds, indulge the mass media, and deliver relief. Of course, all of this has to be done while respecting humanitarian principles.

In the influential book *Disaster Response: Principles of Coordination and Response*, Eric Auf der Heide states,

> One of the reasons disaster response is difficult to coordinate is because *disasters are different from routine, daily emergencies.* Disasters generally cannot be adequately managed merely by mobilizing more personnel and material. Disasters may cross jurisdictional boundaries, create the need to undertake unfamiliar tasks, change the structure of responding organizations, result in the creation of new organizations, trigger the mobilization of participants that do not ordinarily respond to local emergency incidents, and disable

the routine equipment and facilities for emergency response. As a consequence of these changes, the normal procedures for coordinating community emergency response may not be adapted well to the situation.

The field of humanitarian logistics deals with delivering aid and providing relief in situations caused by natural or man-made disasters. Over 35 million people in the world depend on emergency relief to survive in any given year. Every year, more than $6 to 8 billion are spent on relief efforts. During disasters, usually many different organizations attempt to respond quickly while working in settings that are foreign to them. During the past 30 to 40 years, the number of NGOs involved in relief efforts has gone from 938 in 1972 to over 26,000 in 1999.

Orchestrating the humanitarian supply chain is complicated by the need to operate within a humanitarian space, also referred to as the humanitarian triangle. There are three key concepts in the humanitarian space: (a) humanity, which means identifying those in need and helping them; (b) impartiality, which means providing assistance without discrimination and with a priority to those most in need; and (c) neutrality, which means providing aid without bias or affiliation to anyone involved in the conflict. The principle of humanity focuses on maximizing the number of people who benefit from the relief effort. But the principle of impartiality focuses on a weighted benefit—that is, impacting those most in need of relief. Each of these metrics might result in very different choices and deployment strategies.

As an example, in the relief efforts following the floods in Rwanda in 2006, it was only after the relief organizations arrived at the scene that the people most in need were located in border areas. From an evaluation perspective, given the location of the relief supply chain, it may well have failed the impartiality test even if the deployment at the location was successful because the people assisted were based on their location and this implied an affiliation. Similarly, when relief efforts began after the hurricane in El Salvador in 2009, the ruling party was supported by the wealthy segments of society, while the guerilla army was supported by the poorer segments of society. Providing relief required coordination across both segments. The principle of neutrality required preventing any perceptions, apparent or real, that would benefit one or the other political party. Again, the specifics involved with executing the supply chain had to be balanced against the perceived inequities or the impact on the political structure.

In addition to bilateral aid provided directly by donor countries, NGOs usually play a major role in any given humanitarian effort and can have a profound impact on humanitarian logistics. Among others, these NGOs may include the Red Cross, Doctors Without Borders, and World Vision in addition to the United Nations–related entities, such as the World Food Program (WFP), the World Health Organization, the United Nations High Commission for Refugees (UNHCR), and so on. This is in addition to bilateral aid provided directly by donor countries.

The United Nations Joint Logistics Center (UNJLC) is a coordination body within the United Nations (UN) system whose goal is to coordinate logistics across independent agencies from the UN and governmental and nongovernmental organizations (such as the Red Cross). The mission of the UNJLC is summarized as "coordinate but not implement," that is, facilitate the performance of other mission-specific entities but do not get in their way.[1] As relief organizations rush into the location of an emergency, a surge in demand for capacity ensues. There are many steps to be managed. The UNJLC manages permissions from the host country to let individuals arrive, manages congestion, manages coordination with the military or security groups, and so on. Understanding the UNJLC's approach to coordination provides a useful framework to think about orchestrating stretch. For example, when relief organizations were rushing in to provide aid in Afghanistan, a landlocked country, many organizations attempted to enter the country through Uzbekistan and load supplies on barges down the river. The rush by hundreds of relief organizations, each operating independently, created such chaos that the Uzbek government shut down access to Afghanistan. The UNJLC played the role of "traffic cop," debottlenecking the situation by establishing a regular barge schedule and smoothing the flow of aid through the Uzbek entry point. This role of scheduling across independent relief organizations actually increased available capacity and decreased lead time for everyone. Such a coordination role can be considered as *coordination by command,* that is, a centralized scheduler who controls the asset plays the role of an external group that delivers value to all parties, thus coordinating the system and improving performance for everyone. In some stretch contexts, coordination by command involves the creation of a command center where all decision making is centralized. Such a strategy enables a global perspective of the overall performance but requires effective communication from all participants to ensure effectiveness. The downside of such an approach is the prevention of entrepreneurial action—that is, on-the-scene initiative to make the best use of opportunities and the nurturing of perhaps bureaucratic behavior.

Another example is when relief organizations were pouring into Rwanda: The WFP was shipping in food for hungry Rwandans while the UNJLC was shipping out Rwandan refugees from the war-stricken area. Given the floods, the main mode of transport was air. The WFP was flying in food and their planes were flying out empty. The UNHCR was flying in empty planes and flying out full ones. The UNJLC coordinated the schedules across the two agencies so that WFP aircraft flew out refugees while UNHCR aircraft flew in food supplies. The adjustments in flight schedules had to take into account loading issues at both ends, food and refugee arrival at each end, safety and security, and so on. But coordination enabled improved utilization of resources and higher capacity at about the same cost. Such coordination is *coordination by consensus* across relief organizations, each with its own assets. When orchestrating stretch opportunities, there is often the need to work with new partners or across functional areas or divisional lines. In such cases, permitting consensus-based sharing of resources may be the most effective option.

A third example is from Afghanistan, where the UNJLC website provides updates about security and weather, logistics shipment needs (similar to a ride board in most campuses), road conditions, and so on. The ensuing coordination between operating entities is left to individual agencies, who then use this information to seek out interested parties to share resources. Such coordination is minimal; it is left to individual agencies and thus is *coordination by default*. We suggest that in some stretch contexts, where opportunities may be fleeting and may require flexibility to execute, pushing decision making to the lowest levels of the organization with global data sharing may well be the most effective approach. When entering new markets in which resourceful managers have to develop relationships to generate effective performance, such flexibility may be crucial.

These three examples show three different levels of coordination: coordination by command (i.e., a centralized approach), coordination by consensus (i.e., cooperative Pareto improvement solutions in which neither party is worse off), and coordination by default (i.e., no coordination other than perhaps information sharing). A complete theory that matches the optimal coordination type to the situational context remains a research topic at this point (with initial investigations by Iyer and Wassenhove.[2]

A Life Cycle Perspective

Another approach to understanding the evolution of a humanitarian intervention is along the time dimension. The three classic steps in any contingency are ramp up, sustain, and ramp down. During each of these phases, coordination activities consist of deconflicting, debottlenecking, and prioritization and scheduling. As discussed earlier, the varying nature of the scope of the deconflicting and debottlenecking activities suggests different management strategies over the life cycle. It is clear that there will be multiple agencies with individual missions, capabilities, metrics, donors, and so on. Furthermore, the choices made by the owners of the system—governments, ministries, other countries, and so on—create the humanitarian space in which the relief efforts operate. In addition, information may be local and decentralized (e.g., local security, truck rates, contracts, quality of service) or centralized (e.g., weather conditions, road network, satellite images). The resources may be available centrally or donated by agencies, and they may be operated by private agents, the military, or individual relief agencies

During ramp-up, the humanitarian space is unclear, the deployment requirements are urgent, some donors make use of speed of deployment to determine who gets resources (i.e., "the early bird gets the worm" or the "CNN effect"), not too many agencies are there early, and information is fragmented. However, to get the ball rolling requires several one-time tasks to be completed with respect to permissions to operate, taxes on imports, licenses for operating vehicles, rules regarding ownership of goods, clarification regarding laws, visas, landing rights, customs and religious observances, and so on. There may also be infrastructural needs, such as the need for air traffic control, bridges, port clearance from neighbors, and so on. Intuitively, this portion of the deployment life cycle might be best managed using centralized coordination because the number of entities involved may be small and the congestion-related issues critical.

During the sustainment phase, the individual agencies want to operate efficiently but may still require security information, weather information, occasional sharing of resources, help with breaking up cartels, assistance with persistent problems involving interpretation of laws, coordination with military, and so on. Since many parallel efforts may be in operation, with each agency having its own supply chain processes, it may be appropriate to coordinate by consensus

During ramp-down, coordination between agencies would help as they identify local groups to hand over operations to, coordinate with the military for exit, decide how much "development" activity will continue, take actions to prevent mission creep, and so on. Because many entities may be involved and each may be planning a handoff to an appropriate local entity, it may be best to permit independent coordination with information exchanges only.

What can companies learn from humanitarian supply chains? Notice that the same concerns, albeit with different features, occur while orchestrating stretch opportunities even in companies. For example, a supplier's speed of execution has to be balanced against how that speed is accomplished: Are environmental standards being ignored? Are employees forced to work overtime? Are commitments to other customers being violated? In addition, the company has to continue to provide all of its employees with the chance to play a role in this opportunity, follow all existing legal constraints regarding coordinating with competitors, and so on. While some of these concerns are standard during routine operations, stretch opportunities suggest "shortcuts" with a "the end justifies the means" attitude that has to be curtailed. These concerns are similar to issues of humanitarian space. Also, just as in complex emergencies, stretch opportunities usually appear unannounced and require rapid improvisation. Learning from successes across the world thus serves to prevent repetition of failures. After all, one needs to study history to prevent it from repeating.

Summary

Our goal was to provide a quick introduction to the management of humanitarian logistics. We suggest that the frameworks used to study humanitarian logistics provide an effective context to understand organization to attain stretch goals. Coordination by command, by consensus, and by default offer different levels of central direction in guiding execution. Such management choices also reflect possible choices to attain stretch goals. Similarly, a life-cycle view of stretch opportunities mimics the evolution of humanitarian emergencies. In addition, respect for the humanitarian space in an emergency parallels the need to stay within demand for corporate social responsibility. Finally, there is typically a "lessons learned" document at the end of every humanitarian emergency that analyzes performance and suggests improvements. Similar audits will assist continuous improvements in orchestrating stretch opportunities in a commercial environment.

Notice that the processes at work during a humanitarian disaster look quite similar to the processes harnessed when orchestrating a stretch goal. The participants in an organizational stretch opportunity often face unfamiliar territory as far as processes to be followed; there are rapid decisions to be made, resource and financial consequences, and impacts on routine operations. Companies have to be conscious of their ethical standards and brand equity when dealing with stretch opportunities that may generate significant profits.

CHAPTER 7

Fashion Demand Stretch— Everybody Needs a Croc

Globally Scaling a Supply Chain

The shoe company Crocs had its origins in Canada as Waldies, a company that made plastic footwear for gardening. Crocs was founded by George Boedecker Jr. and his friend Lyndon Hanson in 1999. All Crocs-brand shoes were made with a proprietary resin called Croslite. The resin, which is "NOT plastic NOR rubber,"[1] as the company claims, resulted in a particularly comfortable, easy-to-clean, and odor-resistant shoe. The shoes were marketed as suitable for professional and recreational uses such as boating, hiking, hospitality, and gardening. Crocs sold the product without fancy packaging and used an extrusion process to manufacture shoes, thus reducing direct labor. The company did minimal advertising, focusing instead on product comfort and durability and maximizing retail access.

The initial product sales were generated by word of mouth and viral marketing. When first sold under the Crocs name in 2002, they were aimed at boating enthusiasts. There was just one model—a $30 shoe with lots of holes offered in six colors. The company moved early to buy out the manufacturer of Croslite and thus control access to the resin. Next, they signed long-term contracts with suppliers and took control of the supply chain to offer retailers flexibility to place orders and receive quick deliveries of desired colors. The company then moved to making an array of models in scores of colors and started a line of high-end, style-focused shoes that incorporated Croslite.

The Crocs medical line was endorsed by the American Podiatric Medical Association as an alternative to flip-flops. "They started buying them by the hundreds," retailer Gordon Reddick recalls of a medical company near his Wrightsville Beach, North Carolina, shop, which first sold the shoes in basic neutrals: black, white, and brown. "But then people started asking for them in colors. And then the kids came in. And now, well, you don't even want to get near that corner of the store when the new (Crocs products) come in."[2] The word-of-mouth buzz quickly spread. As reports of celebrities wearing Crocs spread—Jack Nicholson was sighted wearing blue Crocs, Faith Hill was seen sporting a tan pair of Crocs, and Britney Spears was reported to have purchased all colors available. Even President Bush was reported to be wearing black Crocs with presidential seal socks.

Colin McDowell reports in his book *Shoes: Fashion and Fantasy* that footwear is susceptible to fads that swing from an emphasis on practicality to appearance. When enough people are wearing one type of shoes, others start wearing them, too—creating a trend. Malcolm Gladwell, author of *The Tipping Point*, describes a tipping point as one that is reached when the levels at which the momentum for change becomes unstoppable.[3] The spread of Crocs is described as a tipping point phenomenon by the blog "Muckle Hen." The process of moving to a tipping point is described by the blog as follows: "One minute nobody was wearing them, then everyone and his wife and all their children were wearing them in a variety of colors depending on what day of the week it was. Shops sprung up that sold nothing else."[4]

Supply Chain Evolution at Crocs

While our discussion has focused on Crocs, it is worth understanding the explosive growth the company managed. A review of their sales growth shows an almost exponential pace from 2003 to 2007.

The founders of the company focused on the material—Croslite—and its antibacterial properties. Their first step was to purchase the supplier of the resin and thus control its availability. Next, they signed contracts with key suppliers to guarantee availability. They focused on sustainable roles for the material while remaining noncommittal about the specific products it would be used for. As soon as demand for the Crocs took off in the United States, executives purchased more manufacturing plants in Canada and Mexico and signed on contract manufacturers in Italy, Romania, and China.

To ensure high-level service to retailers, they focused on lean manufacturing with a quick response to trends. Thus retailers were seldom stuck with inventory, as quick delivery allowed them to adapt to demand trends. Given control of the manufacturing base, the company could be both agile to handle volume changes and flexible in their product line: they make gardening kneepads, dress shoes, hockey equipment such as padding, and specialty shoes for medical patients. The company even planned to offer toilet seats.

As sales grew, Crocs focused on developing a global supply chain. The company built or outsourced to factories in China, India, Brazil, Mexico, and eastern Europe. By locating the supply chain globally, management kept product costs low, thereby holding prices. The supply chain expansion included additional fulfillment and distribution capabilities. Global distribution was facilitated by new distribution facilities in China, adjacent to major third-party manufacturing facilities.

Sales Challenges

While sales were expanding, some stories emerged of customers whose Crocs were getting caught in escalators. Typically, the shoe became entrapped when the rider was stepping on or off the escalator or standing too close to the side. But safety groups in Japan started issuing warnings about soft-sided flexible clogs like Crocs. In Japan, the trade ministry asked Crocs to change the design of its shoes after receiving 65 complaints.[5] The U.S. Consumer Product Safety Commission reported *77 escalator entrapment incidents* in 2006, half of which resulted in injury. All but two of the incidents involved soft-sided flexible clogs and slides such as Crocs, though the company was not specifically cited. The *New York Daily News* reported that a 3-year-old girl wearing Crocs was hurt in an escalator in New York's John F. Kennedy International airport.[6] After noticing an increase in soft shoes getting caught in escalators, the *Washington Metro* posted warnings about wearing soft-soled shoes on escalators. According to the *Pittsburgh Tribune-Review*, Pittsburgh's Mercy Hospital banned workers from wearing Crocs in patient-care areas because they claimed that the holes in the shoes posed a safety hazard.[7] A Swedish hospital banned Crocs-brand plastic clogs because they built up static charges that affected the delicate medical instruments.[8]

Soon Crocs was stumbling badly as shares plunged nearly 45% after officials forecast earnings lower than previous predictions. "With consumers tightening spending, the Crocs' brand isn't strong enough to command prices four times those of its imitations," said retail analyst Keri Spanbauer.[9] The company fired 1,300 workers, mostly in manufacturing, to reduce costs and counter lower sales in the United States. Several factors were reported to slow the rapid growth in the popularity of Crocs, including weaker consumer spending, high market penetration in developed economies worldwide, and competition from similar-looking products and fake Crocs.

Supply Chain Choices and Flexibility, Agility, and Real Options (FAR)

Expansion required Crocs to control their key component—Croslite. Crocs Inc. purchased the company that cooked up the formula for the proprietary resins—Foam Creations in Canada—in June 2004. Until 2005, the resins were compounded in Italy. Crocs expanded with additional compounding facilities. Crocs owns its own manufacturing facilities for the finished product in Canada and Mexico, but about 50% of all Crocs are made in China, and there are also third-party manufacturers in Florida, Italy, and Romania. They realized that controlling distribution would enable them to react quickly to demands for specific colors and assist the retailers in stocking the colors that were in demand. This enabled the price points for the products to be maintained with a low probability of markdowns to eliminate excess inventory. Finally, controlling the resin Croslite would provide the flexibility to evolve products while preventing the competition from getting access to the material.

The rapid expansion of sales meant a high degree of buildup of capacity ahead of demand. This pace worked as long as growth was continual. But a downturn in sales either due to market fatigue or worries about the product's price points, would require Crocs to shift manufacturing and distribution sources quickly. In the downturn phase, the company shut down manufacturing in Canada and shifted it to a plant in Mexico. But they also realized that the markets in Asia were continuing to grow. This required a shift in the distribution to adjust to new market locations.

The banning of Crocs in a couple of hospitals suggested the need to rapidly sense if this would be a trend. Reports indicated that Crocs were used extensively by medical personnel who were on their feet for a major portion of the day. Thus a large negative effect on this group would have a significant impact on demand. This part of their supply chain impact resembles the Kryptonite case—early sensing and an effective alternative focused on this segment would need to be a priority. Similarly, the Japanese government's request to Crocs to change their designs to decrease kids' injuries was a potentially serious demand-shifting event. An effective redesign could enable the Japanese market to grow, particularly since the shoes are mainly used indoors.

At the same time, changing supply chain ownership or use of assets provided a different approach to managing agility and flexibility. Changing ownership of the manufacturing provided capacity utilization relief but potentially could decrease responsiveness to retail orders. Expanding the warehouse to take on tasks for other products might require increased flexibility for warehouse processing. Shifting back to a third-party-operated warehouse provided the same effect. The challenge was for Crocs to use FAR effectively while being mindful of retail expectations for service.

Fast-forward now to 2010, and Crocs managed to decrease its manufacturing footprint and operate at lower cost levels. With increased global distribution, analysts were again forecasting sales growth of over 40%.[10] Increased product flexibility, the agility to respond quickly to order volume changes, and the control of resins all have generated the ability to use FAR to its competitive advantage.

CHAPTER 8

FreeFlow— Stretching the Web

How Technology Enabled Resolution of Supply Demand Mismatches

Imagine a scenario in which you just launched a new product, but your competitor announces an even better technology and goes to market aggressively. Well, you may be holding millions of dollars of inventory that loses value with every breath. A common benchmark in the industry is an 8% price erosion per month. Hence, if a company process deals with obsolescence once every 6 months, it will lose close to 50% of its inventory value. It is clear that a well-thought-out strategy for inventory disposition is vitally important. In this chapter, we will discuss Free-Flow—a company that provides a service to dispose of unwanted inventory effectively.[1]

FreeFlow was founded in 2001 in County Kerry, Ireland, by Alan Scroope. FreeFlow helps companies manage inventory in a unique, cutting-edge, and some might even say *revolutionary* manner. Scroope's vision was to use the Internet to (a) bring competition and transparency to inventory (asset) management, (b) provide operational and administrative services to companies to streamline inventory management processes, and (c) reduce costs. We suggest that FreeFlow provides the capability to manage flexibility and agility by offering another source of demand as a real option—one that can be exercised at will.

FreeFlow is an online marketplace in the business of remarketing excess inventory. The sellers (companies disposing of excess inventory) include companies such as Apple, Microsoft, CISCO, Logitech, Motorola, and 3COM, to name a few. All buyers are preregistered and prequalified, thus giving the seller complete channel control of inventory they are getting rid of. Essentially, FreeFlow is an online private marketplace. It operates at very high velocity; auctions typically run for 72 hours. The majority of revenues are derived from transaction fees (commissions) for inventory sold through the FreeFlow platform. It's an infomediary[2] model that drives added value across the marketplace.

We all know that demand planning and inventory management are not exact sciences. There are always tradeoffs. Whether having too much or too little on hand, having the right mix of stock-keeping units (SKUs) or components, or being able to have a buffer to meet unexpected demand (or lack thereof), companies are constantly struggling to optimize the mix, reduce lead times, and increase inventory turns. Simply put, why tie up cash in inventory that isn't being sold?

Truth be told, companies seldom have a good handle on their inventory. This is due not to a lack of focus or recourse but simply to the complexity of managing thousands of components and finished product SKUs. Most companies deal with inventory obsolescence reactively, not proactively, without a streamlined process for inventory disposal. The world of electronics is particularly vulnerable; price erosion is an important issue, as is the financial risk of sitting on remnant inventory. Think about the speed at which technology changes . . . think about the speed of innovation. The cool smartphone or digital device you bought less than a year ago is practically obsolete today.

FreeFlow has a simple philosophy:

Time is Money . . . and when it comes to inventory asset management, time is not your friend. The pace of new product introduction ensures that price erosion starts just months or even weeks after product launch. Inventory in the channel loses value in direct relation to the cycle of new product introduction. Competitors' product introductions immediately impact the market value of inventory at any stage in its lifecycle.[3]

FreeFlow created a virtual Internet marketplace through which FreeFlow partners have the ability to progressively dispose of their inventory. The FreeFlow technology is a hosted software solution. Partners use the software as a service. It is a completely outsourced solution, which is significant for partners, as information technology

(IT) resources are often stretched and implementation and integration processes for most software solutions can be lengthy and painful. All FreeFlow requires to get going are inventory listings and reserve pricing to be set as desired by partners. It is "plug and play" and can be up and running within days.

In addition to the interface, FreeFlow provides other important services to partners. Scroope believes that with a critical mass of inventory data and visibility of inventory levels and movements in the market, Free-Flow can help companies develop an internal process to concisely and *proactively* identify the areas in which the inventory is at risk by defining price erosion triggers. FreeFlow also helps companies with account receivables and payables by acting as an escrow agent between the seller and buyer.

SanDisk and FreeFlow

Here is a real-life example of how FreeFlow helped a $4 billion electronics manufacturer become more flexible, responsive, and efficient in managing its inventory obsolescence.[4] SanDisk Corporation, headquartered in Milpitas, California, designs, develops, manufactures, and markets flash storage cards used in various consumer electronics products. SanDisk products are used across consumer electronics: digital cameras, mobile phones, gaming devices, laptop computers, other portable devices, digital audio and video players, personal computing devices, network servers, and more. Moreover, SanDisk products are embedded in various systems for the enterprise, industrial, military, and other markets. The company is a global manufacturer with distribution channels in the Americas, Europe, the Middle East, Africa, Asia Pacific, and Japan. Since 2003, SanDisk has enjoyed phenomenal growth: over 300% in just 4 short years, from 2003 to 2007. SanDisk also boasts one of the highest revenue-per-employee ratios in the technology industry. However, SanDisk management had greater plans for the future: in 2005, a strategic plan was put in place to grow revenues to $10 billion, or approximately 5 times what it was then. Being a product development and manufacturing company, SanDisk's vision, which poured down across the organization, was to significantly improve efficiencies, execution, and scalability of its global supply chain. We will not dive into the many cutting-edge initiatives that SanDisk implemented in the areas of demand planning, standard operation procedures, and supply logistics, but we would like to point out how FreeFlow's innovative technology platform helped SanDisk manage (and scale) the inventory disposition process.

For all of SanDisk's product successes, revenue growth, and operational performance improvements, it is not immune to excruciating margin pressure. So in 2004, the company turned its attention to identifying at-risk or excess inventory and moving it through secondary markets, converting idle assets to cash.

Launching more than 20 new products each quarter, SanDisk's supply chain managers had not been able to focus effectively on the constant stream of products that were being made obsolete. The best efforts yielded on average 20 cents on the dollar in recovery, and this in a market with insatiable aftermarket demand for flash memory–based products. And the disposition efforts typically happened only twice a year, when the excess inventory had built up to a point where it began to be a physical obstacle. Why only twice a year? Well, the company simply did not have the bandwidth to manage the process of routinely identifying excess, finding market opportunities, and managing the incremental transaction flow. To address this issue, SanDisk chose to outsource to a specialist in end-to-end asset recovery—meaning everything from at-risk inventory identification; to market research and pricing recommendations; to market creation and identification of buyers; and to final settlement, collection, and other operational issues.

Early conversations with FreeFlow began in the fourth quarter of 2004. By March 2005, FreeFlow and SanDisk agreed on the definition of at-risk inventory and began mapping out the flow of product returns across all three geographic regions: North America, Europe, and Asia Pacific. Over the next 2 months, the inventory asset recovery team—including SanDisk's inventory managers, product specification engineers, product marketers, and representatives from the finance department—thrashed out inventory management policies as well as target pricing and reserve pricing for inventory auctions.

The SanDisk participants sensed a significant opportunity to generate new revenues. For most technology products, price erosion is steep, beginning just months after new product introduction. For flash memory–based products, it can be as high as 15% per quarter. Late-stage inventory is already well down the price curve, making it imperative to have crisp decision-making thresholds, predefined markets, and low-overhead processes. If its disposition process could take place every month instead of twice a year, SanDisk could essentially re-claim two quarters' worth of product value.

FreeFlow set up a monthly series of remote online auctions, facilitating the inventory sale on site at SanDisk's distribution center, with the winning bidder paying the freight cost (previously, SanDisk had incurred shipping costs). With the ubiquitous presence of online auctions (thanks to eBay), SanDisk followed FreeFlow's recommendation to establish a private, branded auction platform for the liquidation of its excess inventory—SanDiskExcess.com—which allows SanDisk to approve the members, the minimum price points, and all bids. Competitive bidding alone—aided by attention to the metric of bid spreads—has shown a consistent performance improvement of more than 30% for SanDisk. On top of that, SanDisk no longer has to spend on marketing promotions, rebates, and other programs usually needed to dispose of surplus inventory.

Throughout, SanDisk used its progressive disposition process (PDP) matrix, developed with FreeFlow, to facilitate review and decision making with respect to excess inventory. The matrix integrates sales, supply chain operations, inventory policy, and product life cycle into a concise, threshold-driven decision-support system. It prescribes a distinct course of action for three categories of inventory:

1. Active and obsolete new inventory still in the company's warehouses
2. Active and obsolete new inventory in the channel
3. Returned inventory, itself broken out into three categories, with "defective" products to be refurbished for resale

For each category, the complete decision-making process, accountability, and action are specified: inventory threshold, product life cycle status, frequency of review, process owner, and disposition action.

So how does FreeFlow add to the flexibility, agility, and real options (FAR) capability of SanDisk? We suggest that FreeFlow provides SanDisk with the real option to dispose of inventory as soon as risk is recognized. Flexibility is maintained by pruning the system of obsolete SKUs, thus permitting focus on current inventory. Agility is provided by permitting scaling of inventory management through a hosted IT system, with FreeFlow absorbing the capacity risk and sharing that risk with all participants. In other words, for the first time, the internet permits the supply chain to capitalize on growth opportunities and realize stretch inventory goals, efficiently.

CHAPTER 9

Orchestrating Reconfiguration

How SAP and Shipwire Enable the Unexpected

When we interviewed several companies, including those mentioned in this book, we discerned that the focus has shifted from efficient to responsive systems and technologies. In fact, managing stretch goals, positioning to act on new opportunities, and being responsive to market fluctuations were the top concerns. In this chapter, we will talk about two representative software companies radically different in scope, mission, and size but both providing cutting-edge solutions to enable customers to manage operational risk and meet stretch goals. One is a giant software enterprise company and the other is a small Silicon Valley technology start-up.

We have all heard of SAP, an enterprise software solutions giant. Headquartered in Walldorf, Germany, with offices in over 75 countries serving manufacturing, financial, and services industries, SAP has long been considered a front-runner in its field. Our mission was to understand how SAP changed from a traditional software solutions company to developing agile and flexible products to accommodate ever changing customer needs.

An examination of BASF, which uses SAP, is illustrative of how this global giant leverages cutting-edge software tools to manage the supply chain. A global player, BASF possesses a complex supply network operating in numerous geographies and incorporating multiple facilities and partners. When unexpected events occur, BASF's assets and supply chain must be reconfigured to service customers efficiently. BASF executives understand that product visibility across the supply chain is fundamental to meeting delivery lead times and keeping customers updated at all times. To become responsive and better manage supply chain risk, BASF implemented SAP event-management software.

The system was put to the ultimate test during Hurricanes Katrina and Rita. Margie Pierce, director of North American Free Trade Agreement (NAFTA) foreign trade and logistics compliance at BASF, said, "In quick succession, two major hurricanes, Katrina and Rita, caused havoc at two of our major ports of entry into the United States. SAP software was instrumental in helping the company meet this challenge."[1] The choreography happened in real time. Everything had to be considered: personnel safety, product vulnerability, security, specific customs handling requirements, delivery of critical components, and many more variables in the complex web of the supply chain equation. Just 24 hours before Katrina hit, BASF management knew exactly what inventory they had on hand, what inventory was on the water scheduled to arrive, and what buffer capacity and rerouting options were available. "We knew which consignments were still in port, which ones were in transit, and which ones had already reached their destination port in Houston or New Orleans. We could therefore take the necessary steps to ensure that our customers suffered as little as possible," explains European project team member Peter Nikolaus.

BASF claims that their SAP event-management software helped orchestrate the reconfiguration of its supply chain in real time while these events were happening. Ships were dynamically rerouted to safe harbors—in some cases several times as the situation changed. BASF's customers were kept informed as the company adjusted its supply chain to maintain its level of service.

To start the conversation, we posed the following question to SAP executives: "How common are requests from your customers for dynamic system reconfigurability?" We learned that such requests are not just common, but in fact they are a de facto communiqué from almost all clients. From a supply chain standpoint, can SAP systems be reconfigured in case of a significant event? We define such an event as an unplanned occurrence that may significantly impact a business, such as an economic downturn or upturn, a new and disruptive technology entering the market, the rise and fall of major competitors, a global political or geopolitical event, and so on. The answer, as a senior SAP employee told us, is that "efficiency is a given, but operational risk is the unknown to reckon with."[2]

SAP separates operational risk into three levels:

1. *Strategic level.* In this top tier, involving network design and plans for resilience, the software provides customers with the ability to run simulations of global events that may disrupt a supply chain (both positively and negatively). Customers can model inventory, manufacturing, distribution, and transportation scenarios to understand the impact on each of an unplanned major shock to the system.
2. *Tactical level.* In this middle tier, clients evaluate short-run strategies, perform impact analyses, and decide whether to respond to or ignore a particular risk.
3. *Execution level.* Finally, this operational tier affords customers the analysis and information needed to meet stretch goals.

SAP provides a slew of solutions, such as event management, detection (sensing a potential issue), and response (tracking in a timely manner through radio-frequency identification [RFID] and other technologies) all the way to batch[3] and lot[4] of products at each level. The software tracks serial numbers at manufacturing and thus provides complete visibility of everything that goes on in the supply chain, from manufacturing, to distribution, to supply logistics, to point of sale. Moreover, this visibility extends beyond a single client into the global movement of goods and services. Putting these SAP product tiers in one cohesive solution set gives clients the visibility and reconfiguration capability to manage stretch goals.

We now know that SAP software can dynamically reconfigure assets across a supply chain in real time, but can it dynamically reconfigure assets when there are changes in a client's processes? This is what clients wanted—the ability to make real-time decisions. The enterprise service-oriented architecture, or ESOA,[5] is the next step. Customers wanted continuous inventory and supply chain replanning and a modularized solution[6] set based on modular services. Therefore, SAP engineers developed a software platform with a composition environment in which a process is composed based on modular services. The software services are reconfigured through an enterprise services repositioning (ESR) tool in a streamlined fashion. Thus, if the process changes, the software can be reconfigured to change as well. Moreover, demand planning options are always exposed and available to marketing and sales management. In other words, with various appropriate permissions rights within the software, a customer can update demand scenarios through an Excel spreadsheet or on a mobile platform, sending data right into the demand planner central tool. Marketers can create dynamic product promotions, with the SAP software providing operations managers with the ability to flex and reconfigure the supply chain based on changes in demand.

In the BASF scenario, SAP provides BASF with flexibility and agility in the actual software to reconfigure a process (product) based on particular activities. These activities can then be reconfigured based on process changes in the event-managements tool, available to BASF. For example, with this tool, BASF monitors ocean freight and has the ability to reconfigure product destination, storage, and delivery across its supply chain.

Let's return to the original question of how a company can orchestrate stretch goals. Naturally, having flexible systems is extremely important. Systems that can be seamlessly reconfigured based on changes in company processes are the future of enterprise resource planning (ERP) software providers. But challenges remain. As many top tier business software giants tackle issues relating to processes, many obstacles will remain unsolved. For example, standards or norms across global supply chains are different, making streamlined and agile solutions difficult to execute. Imagine if all global customers agreed to a unique product identifier, like an Internet protocol (IP) address; movement of goods would become much more transparent and thus potentially easier to reconfigure. Harnessing these capabilities may provide a golden opportunity for software companies to positively affect their clients' businesses.

Let's shift gears and talk about other technologies that are enabling flexible processes. Silicon Valley is teeming with start-ups building technologies to allow agility and flexibility and help companies to scale seamlessly and meet unexpected supply chain events. We have selected one such company to make our point: Shipwire Inc., a venture capital funded Silicon Valley start-up with about 15 employees. Shipwire demonstrates how small, fast-growing companies can leverage the solutions it provides to orchestrate their stretch goals efficiently.

Chris Pallaske, managing director of VoxMicro, expected expansion of his UK wireless products business to take some time and effort, but with Shipwire, he was ready in about 20 minutes. "I could not believe how easy it was to configure," Pallaske says. "It took just a few clicks for us to sign-up with Shipwire, and be ready to manage inventory and shipping." Shipwire's simple administration opened up an easy path of growth for VoxMicro. All inventory management and shipping could now be handled directly on the VoxMicro website, including adding products, sending merchandise, automating order entry, sending confirmation e-mails, and providing order status. "Management is a snap; we even got orders automated from our Web site to the warehouses very quickly," notes Pallaske. As quoted in *Entrepreneur* magazine, "With a virtual warehouse service, all you have to lose are rent and delivery costs."[7]

Founded by Anne Li, AriTrade is an upstart manufacturer of personal windmills and solar panels, providing an alternative energy source for consumers. Little did Li know that her business would quickly win substantial contracts from municipal governments in the United States and internationally—even as far away as India. Then, shortly thereafter, more and more orders started to pour in from green aficionados across North America and Europe. AriTrade's business began to explode. Li's "little" company initially experienced long delays importing components from Asia and shipping them to a warehouse in Manassas, Virginia, for assembly and distribution to customers on the East and West Coast. It all seemed reasonable at the beginning until the volumes grew exponentially overnight. Then Li contacted Shipwire. She immediately plugged into the Shipwire Store-Sell-Ship platform, which provided real-time inventory levels, transportation and fulfillment costs, lead times to customers, and more. With Shipwire, Li was able to locate inventory close to her customers and distributors using Shipwire warehouses in Los Angeles, Chicago, Vancouver, Toronto, and the United Kingdom. Now, when AriTrade receives an order from a West Coast customer, it ships from Los Angeles; when the order comes from France, it ships out of the United Kingdom. It is a hub-and-spokes system, just like a Fortune 500 company. But here is the fascinating part: Li can ramp up to container loads in multiple warehouses and can ramp down to a few pallets in a single center as her demand continues to fluctuate. Shipwire is a month-to-month, pay-for-what-you-use system, so Li isn't burdened by lengthy contracts, leases, or employee commitments. Her storage and shipping resources expand and contract on demand so she can focus on sales and marketing.

The bottom line is that this Silicon Valley start-up can help companies orchestrate stretch goals quickly and efficiently. First, they analyze a company's shipping volume and the location of its customer base. Next, they advise it on the most effective inventory strategy. Shipwire tells the company how many pallets (or even cases) to send to its network partners across the United States and Europe. Then, Shipwire provides order-management software that can quickly integrate with the company's shopping cart. Shipwire developed an open-source applications programming interface (API) to support almost all popular shopping carts. The company's fulfillment is professionally managed, including pick and pack and a choice of a variety of shipping options to suit the needs of its customers. Shipwire customers can access various reports to make sure everything runs smoothly. Finally, Shipwire can provide shipping confirmation, tracking, and so on. Shipwire analytics continuously optimize inventory, fulfillment, and shipping costs while adhering to the agreed-on service levels.

We caught up with the founder and CEO of Shipwire and asked, "What was the 'aha' moment that made you think of starting Shipwire?" The inspiration came from the head of logistics at Costco, who was faced with the challenge of incorporating small regional businesses that contributed to local retail stores into the overall supply chain strategy of Costco. These niche suppliers needed to be managed efficiently and scaled up or down quickly to meet seasonal and promotional demand. Speed and efficiency were top priorities. Hence, the desired solution was a technology to manage fulfillment, shipping, and inventory from a variety of vendors across a variety of products to meet Costco's needs.

It turns out that smaller-size companies are flocking to this new service. Shipwire's technology is an ideal solution to address issues of hypergrowth or the lack thereof. Simply put, scaling fulfillment has become much simpler than ever before. The technology makes it simple and seamless for anyone, anywhere. Imagine running a small Internet business that just exploded with opportunity. Today your company fulfills 100 orders per day, but tomorrow, due to extensive media coverage or a commercial business partnership, your orders jump by 50 times to 5,000 per day. Next thing you know, the holiday season is upon you, and your demand spikes even higher. How can a company with limited financial and human resources manage this? Simple: type in Shipwire.com and get started.

Innovative Web technologies are becoming the go-to solutions for managing not just growth but hypergrowth. They can serve as a reconfigurable buffer capacity, helping small- to mid-sized companies manage unexpected surges in demand, rapid new product introductions, various disaster scenarios, and more. Most important, such technologies provide CEOs with a scalable option to meet unplanned demand quickly and efficiently.

To orchestrate stretch goals, companies need flexible systems. The companies of yesteryear focused on heightened efficiency and the lowest unit cost. Through process optimization driven by systems and software, companies managed to reduce costs and increase profits. But the world has changed: The only certainty of doing business is that it continues to become more and more volatile. What happens when this delicate, fine-tuned systemic balance is disturbed? In previous chapters, we clearly demonstrated that unexpected events happen all the time. These events, if not managed, could be the difference between success and failure. Whether opportunities or threats, they must be acted on quickly and efficiently. It's imperative that systems be agile and flexible, just like organizations and operations of a company. We submit that system reconfigurability to manage operational risk is essential to success. It seems that technology and software industries have gotten the message loud and clear: The customers demand it.

CHAPTER 10

Building Flexibility, Agility, and Real Options Into Your Supply Chain

How Can Your Company Orchestrate Stretch Goals?

If flexibility, agility, and real options (FAR) are the key capabilities to orchestrate stretch opportunities, then how does a company conceptually organize itself to realize these capabilities? Clearly, details will vary with the specifics of the business, but we suggest a few broad approaches that can be developed into operational details and provide specific linkages to examples in this book. First, consider a few drivers of stretch opportunities.

Categories of Stretch Opportunities

The following is a brief summary of demand stretch opportunities:

1. *Significant growth.* Many companies face significant short-term growth spurts or several annual spikes in demand. Take the volume increases described in the Amazon.com chapter (chapter 1). Such volume increases may occur even in mature companies for specific product segments. While the timing of these demand fluctuations may be predictable, the magnitude may not be as evident. Clearly, dealing with spikes in demand and hypergrowth periods requires high system agility.

2. *Product launches.* Many new and exciting products are entering the market, including new toys, cutting-edge computers, new books,

and more. Visualize the logistics challenges faced in distributing more than 450,000 copies of Harry Potter books in a single day after permission to ship was given by the publisher. Imagine using more than 100 airplanes and 9,000 trucks to seamlessly deliver these books at a 40% discount over the list price. Such was the challenge executed by Federal Express and Amazon.com. Again, such temporary spikes in demand require an agile supply chain.

3. *Demand spillovers from external stimuli or competitor failures.* Many decisions made by shoppers are in response to a trend or a recommendation from a credible source. Consider the decision by Oprah's Book Club to feature Toni Morrison's book *Paradise.* This external event triggered an unplanned "run" in demand that had to be managed by booksellers everywhere. Or consider a recent example of companies trying to replace plastics containing bisphenol A with alternatives. Eastman Chemical Company, one of the few suppliers with an alternate technology, faced a significant demand spike as retailers rushed to replace the plastic in their products. Or consider the surge in demand faced by APP Pharmaceuticals, the only company capable of supplying heparin when its competitor Baxter decided to exit the business.

4. *Impact of mergers and alliances.* Many companies grow significantly through alliances and acquisitions. As Amazon.com evolved, the company moved from books, to CDs and DVDs, to toys, to hardware, to appliances, and much more. Such flexibility may be crucial from a strategic point of view but places tremendous pressure on the supply chain.

5. *Disaster-driven stretch.* As disasters strike and products are eliminated, firms have an opportunity to respond to such stretch opportunities and reconfigure their supply chains with the aid of more granular tracking and the rerouting of products. BASF's seamless rerouting in the face of hurricanes, the U.S. Coast Guard's quick setup of communications and response, and Kryptonite's response to blog-driven demand shifts all suggest that disasters and product recalls might create stretch opportunities and companies should be prepared to respond by modifying the supply chain.

What approaches provide FAR capabilities? How do we conceptualize supply chains with high agility? How can we build agility into a supply chain? The following provides a quick list of approaches a company can take to meet stretch goals:

1. *Have on-tap excess capacity.* A classic approach to acquire high agility is to choose a buffer capacity that can accommodate the expected level of demand volatility. Often the cost of being short on capacity is significantly greater than the cost of maintaining the excess capacity. In such cases, buffer capacity provides for agility in the distribution network as well as across the entire system. An example is provided by Jim Kagey, vice president of logistics at Henry Schein Inc.:

   > We plan capacity for the peak season demand and are positioned to meet spikes in demand. We have grown from $800 million to $3 billion in 5 years, with an increase in sales of 65% in 1998. Flexing capacity to meet varied demand was key to maintaining high service levels our customers expect.[1]

2. *Buy a capacity option.* An alternative to building up buffer logistics capability is to have contingent plans to use outsourced capability. The premium paid to an outsourced facility can be viewed as an insurance policy that can be either exercised or forfeited as needed. For example, one of Procter & Gamble's (P&G's) hit products, the "spin brush," was a product that rocketed to over $200 million in sales in just a few months. P&G's product supply strategy was to outsource the production and distribution of this item. Unlike its past product launches, P&G chose to move quickly by outsourcing the "spin brush" supply chain to a third-party provider, thus buying buffer capacity and hedging against increased demand.

3. *Harness company culture.* Another way to absorb swings in demand is to use the inherent flexibility of labor, in which employees literally "flow to the work." A company can develop a culture wherein its labor force is flexible (cross-trained) and can be rotated to assist with any process based on demand requirements. Such labor flexibility enables swings in demand to be handled without explicit buffers (i.e., hiring additional short-term personnel). One example is Reflect.com's decision to position its call center inside the distribution center, thus providing flexibility for customer service representatives to become order-fulfillment overflow support if demand volumes increased unexpectedly. Conversely, distribution

center associates were cross-trained to assist with customer service as required.

How do we think about flexibility? There are several well-known choices that can be used to incorporate flexibility into a supply chain and thus orchestrate stretch opportunities:

1. *Plan for the worst case.* In this approach, we identify the maximum range of stock-keeping units (SKUs) possible and build plans around such a requirement. We call this the min-max rule: Identify the minimum-cost logistics system that can handle the maximum possible product types (variations) the company plans to introduce. How do we think about it from a physical design standpoint? Consider Amazon's choice of adjustable storage mediums (for putting away, picking, and replenishing) that were originally used for books; then for CDs, VHS, and DVDs; then for toys and consumer electronics; and so on. The designers of Amazon's distribution network didn't know what products were coming or when. They did know, however, that dissimilar products were coming. Therefore, the designers planned for the "worst" case: First, build for initial use and then reconfigure for future use without sacrificing productivity. Such a design represents an investment in flexibility, permitting the logistics system to handle a variety of future products, while preparing for unknown contingencies.

2. *Design flexible resources.* In such an approach, we plan the deployment of every resource in a multitude of ways. In the manufacturing domain, Igus Manufacturing epitomizes flexible design. Their plant design has features that enable rapid modifications "on the fly," such as exposed overhead electrical wiring that allows for easy access and few obstructive support columns. The plant design enables Igus to expand, shrink, or relocate entire departments in response to the products being produced.

3. *Have a portfolio of capabilities.* This approach anticipates that additional capacity may be required in the future and thus builds in the ability during the initial design to deploy the appropriate capacity through effective profiling. Such a hybrid choice was made by Amazon's operations team in 1998–1999. A highly automated hybrid

distribution design (split case,[2] full case,[3] and off-line product handling capability[4]) was approved and implemented by Amazon. Through this flexible design and its equipment choices, Amazon was (and still is) capable of flexing capacity to meet increased demand and continuing to branch into dissimilar products.

Summary

While several detailed processes are involved in orchestrating stretch, this chapter offers management several approaches to optimize the responsiveness of the supply chain. Given the wide variety of stretch opportunities bound to confront any given business, company leadership should anticipate that stretch-driven performance will be the norm rather than the exception. The lists discussed previously can help a business develop new strategies for dealing with unexpected demands requiring agile and flexible responses. Moreover, an organization must preemptively nurture within its existing structure a culture of ingenuity and nimbleness to effectively execute the real options discussed throughout this book. In short, an organization should be prepared to orchestrate stretch if for no other reason than it is a key ingredient in any organization's competitive arsenal.

CHAPTER 11

Gizmo—A Story of Stretch

Stretching a Fictional Story of Success

Gizmo's CEO Max Zen was looking forward to a much-deserved retreat with his senior executive team. He eyed the sunset over Puget Sound from his office in downtown Seattle. Although small, the office had a spectacular view of the Olympic Mountains and Puget Sound. The sky was uncharacteristically clear, and the mountains seemed crisp and resolute in their grandeur. Max took a deep breath. Yes, Jackson Hole, Wyoming, was a fabulous setting for getting the leadership team together. The 3-day retreat was planned meticulously, including strategic work sessions, prominent guest speakers from academia and industry, gourmet food, select wines, and the pièce de résistance: 18 holes at the famous Teton Pines golf course.

However, more than the retreat itself, Max was looking forward to the 1,022-mile journey on his Harley Road King Custom. The rigors of being the CEO and chairman of a fast-growing publicly traded company were immense. Yes, he needed to think, switch off, get away from the Blackberry, and reflect on the successes of the past and the challenges of the future. The theme of the conference was "Orchestrating Stretch Opportunities": Max wanted to position the company to take advantage of unexpected opportunities in the years to come. The industry was exploding with innovative technologies, yet the markets were filled with uncertainty. Where would the growth come from? Gizmo's investors were hungering for continued double-digit growth, yet planning for such growth was most difficult in the current climate. Hence, being ready for the unexpected and taking advantage of small windows of opportunity were key. That's what this alone time was for.

Max awoke at the crack of dawn on Saturday morning. The scheduled departure for Jackson Hole was 8 a.m. Everything was ready. Helmet strapped, shades securely in place, he started his bike. An unmistakable deep guttural rumbling of his Harley filled the garage; he kicked the bike into gear and took off.

Although Max already had a framework in mind for his address, over the next 2 days, he was hoping to gather and harness his thoughts. As the crisp air rushed past his face, his mind cleared. He would start with a story of the lessons learned by Gizmo over the years. Then he would frame and summarize Gizmo's upcoming challenges. Finally, he would ask the team to think about the stretch opportunities of tomorrow and how to achieve them.

Gizmo's History

Max recalled how it all began with an observation and a few thoughts. He and his best friend from high school, Jake, were sitting around dreaming of greatness as they got ready for their first jobs out of college.

"I love listening to music," Max said, "but I hate buying all those CDs for $15 a pop. Plus, I don't have room to store them all!"

"Yeah, I hear you," said Jake. "There are other problems, too. I can never find the song I want to listen to, and most of my CDs get scratched quickly, so it's a waste of money. And by the way, I hate when I buy a CD for a single song and get stuck with 10 other tracks that are terrible."

"Yep, very true" said Max. "But what if there were a technology that could somehow digitize all the music, maybe even movies and stuff . . . and then a device could be invented to keep them on? For example, this gizmo could also be used as a phone, a PDA or PC, a device where I could watch a World Series game . . ."

"Very interesting," said Jake. "A device that can do it all and still fit in your pocket? The company that invents and produces something like that will rule the world." The two friends laughed emphatically, but this was no joke. The light bulb went on . . . and that's how during one hot and humid August evening the idea for Gizmo was born.

Later that year, Max read in a technical journal about a researcher who developed a revolutionary mini capture-compression technology that showed tremendous promise. Max decided to contact the researcher.

After a few e-mails and phone conversations, Max set up a breakfast with Leonid, the mastermind of the new technology, to learn more. The conversation lasted almost until lunch. It seemed that the technology was a true breakthrough on a scientific level. Leonid had applied for and received a broad patent and therefore owned this unique and promising intellectual property. Max did not share his business idea with Leonid but simply focused the conversation on the technology itself.

After Max's meeting with Leonid, every waking moment was spent thinking about the opportunity. He and Jake were in constant communication. Next, the two entrepreneurs agreed to do a little market research. Jake was the expert. The two wanted to validate a few assumptions: Is the concept of an all-purpose portable device appealing to consumers? If so, why? Is there a market? If so, how big? What product features are most attractive and which are not? What are consumers willing to pay for it? The two friends wanted to get market validation before writing a business plan. They received it, big time. They ran a quantitative study that suggested a very high purchase intention for the would-be device. In fact, the purchase intention measured at 75%! This meant that 75% of consumers they surveyed said they would *definitely* buy such a device.

Adjusting these assumptions to be a bit more conservative, they developed a business plan. Jake wrote the marketing section and Max completed the financials and product-development assumptions. The two brought Leonid into the fold and offered him a substantial equity stake in the future company. In return, Leonid agreed to license the intellectual property (IP) to the company. With the initial investment from friends and family and a few angel investors, the journey began, and a Delaware C corporation was born. The two decided to name it Gizmo Inc.

Max suddenly became aware that he felt chilly and was a little hungry. He had traveled about 3 hours. The plan was to stop in Coulee City, Washington, and stretch his legs along the shores of Lake Banks. A few miles later, Max pulled into a small sandwich shop and ordered a hoagie, a bag of chips, and a diet soda. He reached Coulee in a few more minutes and then followed the signs to the lake. Soon thereafter, Max was sitting on the side of the lake with his feet feeling the clear, icy waters of Lake Banks. He bit into his hoagie and again was lost in thought.

What made Gizmo such an early success? Undoubtedly, it was a great product called the Gizmo. "Ah, yes," thought Max. "If only people knew how challenging it was to design and manufacture a highly innovative, breakthrough consumer product." How did Gizmo do it? By stretching innovation to its limits. Max and Jake clearly understood that a multipurpose, all-in-one device would be very difficult to develop. The engineering problems were vast and the manufacturing process and quality controls were extremely complex. Moreover, sourcing a variety of custom components was challenging and quite expensive. The early thought was to build a simple device able to deliver basic functionality. "What if we built a great music device that fits in the palm of your hand?" thought Max. Less complexity and a faster time to market seemed like a good idea. But Jake disagreed. There were dozens of similar devices that, while maybe not as cool as the promise of Gizmo, were popular with consumers and widely adopted by the retail channels of distribution. He maintained that the power of the Gizmo brand was acutely tied to the multipurpose design: an all-in-one, slick-looking device that was a phone, music and video player, calendar, Web browser, and more. It was a great vision but rife with challenge.

Max and Jake worked to assemble a great team of executives. Leonid took on the job of vice president of product development and Sanjay Gupta was hired as the vice president of operations. Gizmo's vision was a device that could be customized based on consumer preferences and based on actual demand. The answer was a modular product design, starting with a base unit and a variety of compatible components, that would become a plug-and-play consumer device. Consumers would choose functionality based on what they could afford.

Their approach was clear: First, the products were engineered as one complete device with all the components and plug-ins included. Then, like an onion, the layers were peeled off, stripping the device to its basic core. The reasoning was simple: By creating a top-down approach, all components would be compatible. The design strategy worked flawlessly. The second piece of the stretch innovation was manufacturing. Clearly, Gizmo could not afford large stockpiles of inventories of hundreds of stock-keeping units (SKUs). The working capital needs would be staggering and they knew that cash was king. The out-of the-gate solution was outsourced, modular manufacturing. Sanjay was able to negotiate a cost-plus deal on extra capacity with several premier contract manufacturers. With this solution, Gizmo could use the established facilities, equipment, and processes of a reputable manufacturer and simply pay a small surcharge for using excess capacity. Gizmo used plant labor resources as needed, again paying a small management surcharge to the plant. What Sanjay received in return was complete agility of equipment use and flexibility of labor. Gizmo was also able to control quality and innovate. Gizmo created a manufacturing research and development (R&D) lab, to develop new assembly techniques and thus reduce lot size efficiently. This was a win-win: extra revenue for the manufacturer and micromanufacturing capabilities for Gizmo without actually investing in building a plant. It was a breakthrough the company needed to be profitable.

The third problem Sanjay had to solve was with the supply chain itself: how to work efficiently with suppliers, manufacturers, distributors, transportation companies, and so on. Again, the logistical problem was due to the mass-customization strategy at Gizmo. After all, the products did not exist until the consumer created them. Well, that was not exactly the case, but that's how Max and Jake wanted to position the brand. In reality, the way Sanjay framed the problem was as follows: Initially, there were three core devices that allowed different modular plug-in applications to be connected to the core unit. All three had digital telephony capabilities. One was mainly compatible with audio, video, gaming, and streaming media; they called it "The Little Dipper." The other was mostly business focused, with an integrated operating system (OS) platform to run all business applications, including push e-mail, a wireless LAN sync, a browser, various input and output ports . . . in another words, the world's smallest PC. They called it "The Big Dipper." The third was an all-in-one device that did it all. Jake called it "The Milky Way Galaxy." Then there were 13 plug-in modules to the 3 core devices that allowed the base units to function as consumers wanted them.

Finally, in addition to the functional device choices, Gizmo would offer late-stage customization in 3 forms: device colors, client-designed back plates, and even etched inscriptions on the device. To start, 6 colors would be available for each custom Gizmo. Then Jake wanted a more compelling custom experience. He wanted consumers not just to be able to select a device color but to design the back plating. Jake wanted to offer 12 design permutations. For the "techno" crowd, Jake came up with the Matrix-type bits-and-bytes layout; "gadget lovers" received design noir, filled with abstract gadget images and so on. Lastly, consumers would be able to etch personalized inscriptions, up to 20 characters, on the back of their devices. Gizmo's supply chain had to have the capability to process orders for more than 2,000 possible SKU permutations. All SKUs needed to be assembled a few at a time based on actual demand and be delivered to consumers' mailboxes in 5–7 business days.

To succeed, Sanjay needed to work closely with Jake and his team. One final question remained: How would consumers build this device? How would they select components that were just right for them? The solution was to build a very smart website with a user interface that put consumers in control. A complex set of decision trees were created to profile the clients and help them select the perfect product. Finally, through a Web experience consisting of a combination of visual and textual cues, consumers selected features and components important to them and were able to create their perfect devices. Once created, the site allowed consumers to customize their devices further. Clients decided on appearance choices that met their lifestyle needs.

This website turned out to be hugely popular. The experience amplified Gizmo's brand promise and became the catalyst for strong sales. The key ingredient that tied everything together was an information technology (IT) system that allowed real-time information flow across the entire supply chain and back to the website. But that was another story . . .

The Christmas Stretch

Max smiled to himself. Orchestrating stretch innovation was the catalyst for Gizmo's early success. They did it by taking risks and breaking a few rules in product design, being flexible with manufacturing, and driving agility in every supply chain process. The mass-customized approach was the undiscovered territory, and skeptics said, "It's impossible," "It has never been done successfully," and "It will take too long and cost too much" . . . but they did it! Gizmo launched a killer product with a unique consumer-centric value proposition in just 10 months. The answer was *agility* of process, supply chain, and systems; *flexibility* of thought processes, culture, and decision making; and *real options* created from unique capabilities driven by Gizmo's innovative approach.

The mass-customized Gizmo products were a huge hit. Everyone had to have one. The orders were growing at an alarming rate. Gizmo's primary distribution channel was online, a logical place to be for a mass-customization company. However, the company had plans to expand into different channels the following year, beyond the online environment where Gizmo was growing exponentially. Plans were being developed to enter retail and catalog channels. The channels were also expanding into education, government, and business-to-business (B2B) channels the following year.

Suddenly, Max snapped back to reality. A painful memory forced itself to the forefront of his brain. He recalled how the company almost died a quick death—as quick as it attained success, it almost ceased to exist. Yes, during its 3rd year of operation, Gizmo was approaching the holiday season. The business was growing at an alarming pace. Jake and the marketing team were on front pages of many major trade magazines; they were flying high. Frequent after-work celebrations and office parties accentuated Gizmo's brand awareness and sales volume success. On the other hand, Sanjay and his team were completely underwater. The growth was very difficult to keep up with. Scaling the supply chain was becoming a real problem. One Saturday in September, Max was out with his wife for an evening of dinner and theater. The two just saw a terrific of production of Molière's *School for Wives*, one of Max's favorite plays. On the way home, Max decided to stop by the office to pick up an extension cord for his PC, which he forgot to bring home. He walked in at 11:10 p.m. and found Sanjay and most of his team there working. Max was stunned. He promptly ordered everyone to go home immediately and vowed to get to the bottom of this on Monday. He felt out of touch. He felt that something was wrong.

On Monday morning, he called his senior leadership team for a meeting. They went over the numbers and metrics from all areas of the company. The analysis was both positive and disturbing. The sales growth was a positive, but they were falling behind in keeping up with on-time delivery and their consumer promise. They were still within acceptable levels, but the trend was showing a steady decline. Max asked Sanjay to prepare capacity utilization scenarios to be presented to him and the team on Wednesday. Max wanted to understand three scenarios: (a) the current plan, (b) an accelerated Christmas plan, and (c) a stretch plan if demand exceeded all expectations. What was the absolute maximum number of orders that Gizmo could fulfill on an average holiday day?

The problem was serious. Gizmo's brand equity was two-fold: customized superior products and superior service. Max had no major concern about the product. But not meeting consumer delivery promises during the holiday gift-giving season could be disastrous. Imagine receiving your Christmas gift at the end of January. Max needed to understand the risks. Negative public relations (PR) and lost consumer confidence would kill the brand.

Wednesday morning, Sanjay and the operations management team were ready to present the data. According to Sanjay, the team planned for a doubling of demand. However, with certain modifications in equipment and processes, operations could possibly handle a maximum of 2.5 times the orders from an average September shipping day. "Anything beyond that was impossible," said Sanjay. "We can't build or lease buildings, install equipment, hire and train labor, and ramp up efficiencies in less than 2 months. We live in a physical world where things take time." A brief silence followed.

"That's not acceptable," Max said. "Although we have not planned such an explosive growth to date, it's happening. Thus I believe Christmas volume will also be bigger than planned. I would estimate at least 4 times the current demand—twice the amount of the current plan. We need to stretch our minds and get it done. Failure is not an option."

Max was suddenly aware that he was smiling. The tight-fitting helmet was digging into his cheekbone. Maybe grinning within a tight-fitting full-face helmet was not a good idea. He composed himself. The ride was peaceful: not much traffic and occasional small towns and main streets lasting less than a mile. He was in eastern Washington: sparsely populated country with good folks and lots of open spaces. As he enjoyed his Zen moment, he pushed on.

The team agreed that Gizmo had one intangible asset that could snatch victory from the jaws of defeat: a great organization committed like no other. From the beginning, Max insisted that all employees become shareholders of the company. At company meetings, he often told a story he heard at a Christmas party years ago. One of his friends, an associate professor at a prestigious university, took a sabbatical in India for 9 months. During that time, she decided to rent out her house. Well, as the story goes, the renters wrote shopping lists on the wall in permanent marker, nailed a Christmas tree right to the parquet floor, and more.

Now, no owner would ever do that to his or her wall or living room! The question Max posed to Gizmo employees after telling this story was this: "Would you do these things to your house? Of course not! Well, you are all owners of Gizmo, so treat this company as if it's your own home!" Gizmo had a strong "can-do" culture. Everyone was ready to do whatever it took to succeed. The other thing that made Gizmo's work-force unique was its "on-boarding process." Every employee had to spend one full week either at the distribution center (DC) or at a manufacturing and assembly plant. Every employee had to be cross-trained in every operational process: For example, in the distribution center, employees trained to receive, stock and put away, pick, consolidate orders, pack, and ship. During DC training, newly hired "Gizmopods" (a way Gizmo employees referred to each other) reported to the DC at 8 a.m. on Monday morning. They were given a 1-hour detailed overview of a particular DC process and were then paired up with an experienced DC employee for hands-on learning. The apprentices would then perform actual daily tasks while improving their accuracy and productivity. Moreover, Gizmo policy stated that once every 12 months, every employee (including the CEO) had to work at least one full shift at the DC or assembly plant. Interestingly enough, the reason for this mandatory exposure to the operations was not to build cross-trained operational skills but to drive a culture of cohesion and inclusion. The original idea was that all Gizmo-pods were united in their vision and no one person was bigger or better than anyone else. Unbeknownst to Gizmo, they had created an incredible asset: a cross-trained, flexible labor force that could shift effectiveness based on the business's needs. This became the first pillar of Gizmo's operational stretch goal success.

The second pillar was space—yes, simply space. The plan Max and the team agreed on was as follows. To begin, the operations team carefully studied the production throughput scenarios, optimizing the throughput of each individual operational process. Then the team scaled processes by simply allocating more space for staging, picking, packing. First, the operations team erected a climate control tent in the employee parking lot in one of the two Gizmo DCs. The tent was dubbed "The Cirque" after *Cirque du Soleil*. The Cirque gave Gizmo an additional 18,000 square feet of space. Employees were encouraged to park in a rented lot 2 miles outside the DC, and Gizmo provided a 24-hour shuttle to and from the temporary lot. Second, taking advantage of the high ceilings in the DC, the operations team contracted with a company to build an 8,000-square-foot mezzanine floor right above the receiving area. The vendor agreed to complete the construction in under 4 weeks. Both the Cirque and the mezzanine were quickly converted into additional staging and processing areas, allowing for greater capacity and throughput. Finally, the shipping docks were also extended, and pallets and bins of packages were staged in trailers, waiting for the transportation companies to pick them up.

These simple strategies increased throughput by 31%. Moreover, Gizmo optimized the existing DC layout to free up additional processing space, thus increasing throughput another 11%. All three shifts were now staffed at 100% capacity with Gizmo DC and non-DC employees. Gizmo added a third shift, known as the graveyard shift. This shift was primarily staffed with senior managers, directors, and other Gizmo executives; at Gizmo, management always led by example. Moreover, Gizmo had another DC in Pennsylvania that serviced East Coast customers. This DC was larger, more modern, built for future growth, and had plenty of extra space. However, Gizmo did not have offices in Pennsylvania and therefore no support from local overflow labor. To solve this problem, Gizmo took 200 volunteers and put them on a charter flight to Pennsylvania, where they stayed and worked relentlessly for 6 weeks during the holidays.

Next, Gizmo took more financial exposure, or risk, on finished goods inventory. Through flexible procurement systems, electronic data interchange (EDI), and supplier intranet technologies, Gizmo took an aggressive inventory position to make sure they didn't run out of components to make products. The suppliers were stretched to the limit. Gizmo even paid a higher price to expedite manufacturing and delivery of certain SKUs. The finance and risk management departments had a clear mandate to shift from "business as usual" to management of stretch goals as efficiently as possible. In essence, Gizmo hedged a potential of increased sales during the holidays by investing in more inventory. Although the hedge had cash flow implications, there was no huge risk from the standpoint of profitability; Gizmo had many levers to increase sell-through of various components, even if the holiday demand was less than expected.

Finally, the IT department had to stretch and perform with excellence. The website would have to handle 5 times the traffic and orders.

Order management, warehouse management, and other back-end systems would be stretched beyond tested capacity. Gizmo's chief information officer (CIO) had to act quickly. The IT team immediately began optimizing Gizmo's infrastructure and applications. Hardware and telecommunications vendors were able to help by adding extra capacity and fine-tuning load balancing across all servers. The applications team had implemented monitoring tools and a specific "throttling" code, which enabled them to manage surge capacity. This code allowed IT to set the upper limits of given systems processing capabilities. Therefore, once the upper limit was reached, IT could actually stop the flow of new transactions until the existing transactions were processed. In essence, Gizmo would actually close its website to consumers for a short time until systems could handle more demand.

This was an unprecedented turn of events. None of these tactics were planned. What made it work was a great culture, decentralized and streamlined decision making, flexible systems, and old-fashion hard work. Max recalled the metrics—somehow they were forever embedded in his brain. Perhaps giving dozens of interviews on the subject had something to do with it. On an average day in September, Gizmo shipped 24,000 orders. On an average December day, just 2 months later, Gizmo shipped an average of 109,000 orders. Amazingly, on Tuesday, December 16, Gizmo DCs shipped 132,000 orders—an incredible increase of 550%! Yes, they did it. They stretched beyond their actual capability and succeeded.

New Stretch Opportunity

Max stopped right after sunset at a small, nondescript town near Missoula, Montana. After a simple dinner and a long, hot shower, he was asleep. The next day, Max planned to get an early start. He had 380 miles to cover to get to Jackson Hole. The ride was going to be spectacular. He was hoping to reach Yellowstone before midday. The weather was perfect: cool, crisp, and sunny. As he took off and accelerated to a comfortable speed, once again he was lost in thought.

He recalled hiring a boutique consulting firm to help drive Gizmo's innovation process in a structured manner. During one of the *ideation* sessions, the consultant raised an intriguing idea. He described the similarity between Gizmo's flexible manufacturing and product design and the automotive industry. Could individual components of a car be "smart enough" to communicate with one other? In other words, instead of the mechanical integration of components, could digital signals govern how the engine performed? Some Japanese automakers had already replaced the automatic transmission with an electronic signaling component, which allowed for better fuel consumption and an almost 20% reduction in manufacturing costs. By decreasing the number of physical components, the car would be easier to optimize and faster to manufacture. Thus an effective integrative signal device would have a lot of potential. The consultant seemed to be very enthusiastic about Gizmo's engineering prowess and ability to bring such a product to market. He maintained that engineering and R&D were core competencies at Gizmo, hence giving the company a competitive advantage to develop new products and enter new markets. But venturing into the automotive industry was certainly an incredible stretch opportunity.

Max's plan for the management off-site meeting was to get all his senior executives to focus on this challenge for the entire day. Gizmo's core business was growing and very profitable. However, Gizmo's technology had many other applications. Could Gizmo reinvent itself as a central player in the automotive industry? Perhaps with an acquisition and an investment in R&D Gizmo could repurpose its core technology to revolutionize the automotive manufacturing process. Imagine patenting and licensing a technology that could create more fuel efficient vehicles at a 20% lower manufacturing cost.

Max wondered if his executives would be overwhelmed by the challenge of thinking about a completely different industry. If he could get everyone focused on products that would enable Gizmo to capitalize on its history, Gizmo would get to orchestrate stretch opportunities yet again. To help rationalize and frame this opportunity with his team, Max had a "secret weapon": Rafael Chang. His story would surely inspire the troops and draw important parallels to frame the opportunity Max had in mind.

Rafael Chang's Story at Logflow Inc.

Max and Rafael met a long time ago during their undergraduate days. The two had lost touch for years only to be reunited by a chance encounter last year at a technology conference in Las Vegas. They had dinner that evening and spent time swapping stories and catching up.

Rafael had several business achievements to his credit. A recent cover article in *Business Ventures* magazine summarized how he grew Logflow Inc., his most recent venture, from a 5-person operation to a successful business with over 400 people in little over 2 years. His knack for seizing opportunities and delivering results was legendary in the Silicon Valley. Logflow had started with the premise that most companies are organized for routine flows that generate stable revenues requiring a focus on efficiency. But most companies also understood that growth and profitability had to come from a "carpe diem" attitude, not just efficient operations. It required rapid assessment of opportunities and effective orchestration of supply chain stretch goals. To that extent, Logflow had created a unique methodology and a systematic approach that provided both organizational capability enhancements and transactional flow-through for unplanned events and unforeseen opportunities.

Rafael related Logflow's newest accomplishment—their role in assisting a company in Mumbai, India. An opportunity to be a keynote speaker at an emerging markets conference brought Rafael to Mumbai. It all began at a breakfast meeting with Kishen Lal. An enthusiastic young MBA and scion of one of Mumbai's prominent industrialist families, Kishen had recently managed to acquire the Indian rights for a novel way to manage phone calls seamlessly between the Web, cell phones, and landlines. Eager to scale up quickly and capture market shares, Kishen sought the meeting with Rafael after reading about the introduction of synthetic heparin, which had been a global fiasco until Logflow stepped in. In just 6 months, Logflow managed the manufacture, launch, support, and global distribution of synthetic heparin under the Logflow brand. Since the customary global supply of organic heparin had been disrupted, Logflow came out as a huge winner, gaining significant market share in no time at all.

Kishen posed a question to Rafael: Would Logflow be interested in managing his technology in India? He minced no words when he described the cell phone market in India, which was growing faster than in any other country but was a hypercompetitive market with the world's lowest communication rates. In most parts of India, a call cost 1 rupee (or 2.5 cents) with no charges to receive calls. This meant that any alternative service provider not only had to be cost efficient but had to provide novel capabilities. What could Logflow do to assist? Should this be a business that Logflow could develop in return for a stake in the venture? Could Logflow's managerial capability and novel approach be transported from the United States to Mumbai and the rest of India?

Rafael took lots of notes. His mind was racing with questions. Could the capabilities of Kishen's technology be purchased from providers who could be paid on a per-usage basis? What strategic capacity had to be procured so that growth would not be bottlenecked? Could that capacity be sourced worldwide, or did it have to be locally available in India? And what about the unique handsets that had to be provided to enable customers to use this technology? How would that hardware be produced and distributed?

Rafael recalled having read about the success of Bharti Telecom, an Indian company that outsources its IT to IBM, its switches to Ericsson and Alcatel, its hardware to Nokia, and its analysis to SAS while controlling the brand. An article in the business press claimed that out of every 1-rupee phone call, Bharti made a 40%–50% gross margin and distributed the remaining money to all of its outsourced providers. This novel strategy reversed India's historic reputation as an outsourcing destination rather than as a source. An article in the *Foreign Affairs Quarterly* by Sam Palmisano, CEO of IBM, described Bharti Telecom's novel approach to knitting together services provided by specialist companies in a hypergrowth environment.[1] The article described how firms were specializing in their tasks and were focusing on slivers of the supply chain that could be performed in a location that provided the best mix of cost and quality. Banks, insurance companies, manufacturing facilities, professional services, and R&D firms located in India, China, Australia, and the Philippines focused on specific services. Chipmakers in Korea and Taiwan used U.S. engineers for their manufacturing know-how. Customer service centers in Nova Scotia handled warranty claims processing for U.S. customers. Radiologists in Australia read X-rays for U.S. doctors. Shared standards enabled plug-and-play use of such services within existing supply chains. He cited the need for innovation and integration to drive new supply chain networks of such global specialists. Could Logflow manage Kishen's company using a similar strategy?

By the time he left at the end of the week, Rafael had all but decided that Logflow had to be stretched again—the opportunity in India seemed like a great test case. Logflow would start in Mumbai, India's business capital. Stretching in Mumbai would require resilience, careful choice of partners, and cost management—capabilities that Logflow had. Rafael knew well that given the vagaries of India's markets, the company might make its money through new opportunities. Any design choices thus had to preserve flexibility, agility, and real options that could be exercised as events unfolded. Recalling the story of Logflow was somehow exhilarating. There were interesting lessons to be learned. Moreover, these lessons seemed much more appropriate in light of the challenges Gizmo was currently facing.

Max passed Island Park, Idaho, and was just minutes away from West Yellowstone. The terrain was starting to get a bit more rugged but also more beautiful. His thoughts drifted back to Rafael and Logflow.

After returning back to his Bay Area office, Rafael and his team pondered the opportunity to manage Kishen's technology company. There were many things to consider. To start, Logflow's team decided that the core corporate staff of the management company would be housed in Singapore, close to the manufacturing location of the computer hardware required to run the company. Singapore had a reputation as a business-friendly environment where intellectual property would be protected and commitments were kept by the government and by suppliers. It also provided a great hub of operations, with several IT firms located in the country. Locating in Singapore would also permit a global reach as the service rolled out across a global customer base.

The key to Kishen's strategy was for Logflow to efficiently coordinate the efforts of all the individual providers to enable the company to scale. But to guarantee that new customers would be delivered a seamless experience, Rafael suggested that Logflow set up its own operation to make sure it could orchestrate seamless coordination to provide services to customers who desired surge capacity. As soon as these new customers had more predictable volume forecasts, they would be migrated to a coordinated supply chain, which would be easier to manage and control. Such a two-pronged strategy of servicing both new and established clients offered Kishen's company the ability to guarantee service for customers while enabling and maximizing efficiencies once volumes stabilized.

Logflow's patented software technology would monitor customer demand and adjust Kishen's company's assets to maximize performance and efficiency. Fine tuning the technology and its implementation required Logflow to dedicate a team to install it and make necessary adjustments based on a feedback loop to and from the customer. Moreover, Logflow account managers required a direct link to service providers and managers in Kishen's operation to quickly fine-tune any deviation in the system in real time. To reach optimum performance of seamless integration between customers, service providers, Kishen's operation, and Logflow's technology, Rafael had also asked that his team be involved in (a) negotiating terms of service with suppliers, (b) assisting with establishment of task management protocols with service partners, and (c) service-partner training to use Logflow's tools and techniques to ensure a seamless client experience.

The Logflow-assisted transformation of Kishen's idea was heralded in the business press as an innovative and cutting-edge approach to third-party strategic management. Several academics had stumbled onto this story and were pressing to know more about Logflow's approach and technology. But Rafael remained coy and let his clients do the talking.

Kishen's dramatic business volume increase servicing Indian markets enabled Logflow to grow from a 10-person operation to one with more than 150 people in just 5 months. Rafael even pondered writing an article in *Foreign Affairs Quarterly* to describe his experience with globalized commerce and stretch opportunities.

Naturally, Rafael's story was a great metaphor for Gizmo's future challenges. Max saw a common thread linking Gizmo's management experiences and Logflow's successes.

Learning From Success

Max was approaching his destination. Although the ride was mentally relaxing, his body was tired. He needed to rest. He went over in his mind the chronology of events for the next few days. They would begin the management retreat with a Gizmo history lesson. Learning from past successes and failures was important. He would then introduce Rafael Chang and have him explain how Logflow succeeded in India. The seamless orchestration of technology, suppliers, market demand, and consumer service in the most challenging environment imaginable seemed like a good case study to learn. He would discuss Gizmo's most recent results and the focus of the year ahead. To examine future opportunities, he would leave his managers with the unique auto-industry challenge and opportunity for stretch that Gizmo could seize. Yes, seize.

Finally, he would end with the common-denominator principles of managing unexpected opportunities: *FAR*.

1. *Flexibility* of labor, both at Gizmo and its suppliers
2. *Agility* of the supply chain and technology
3. *Real options:* Gizmo's ability to create an environment where real options exist and management could shift focus, resources, finances, and the supply chain configuration to orchestrate stretch opportunities *efficiently*

Building a culture of FAR was Max's greatest achievement at Gizmo. The culture enabled the company to do unprecedented things. *Flexibility, agility, and judicious use of real options were the secret to Gizmo's success— that and a great organization capable of turning on a dime.* At the conclusion of his presentation, he would leave his senior executives with time to generate a plan for Gizmo to seize the opportunity in the auto industry and stretch the supply chain once again.

CHAPTER 12

Book Summary, Conclusions, and Takeaways

A Summary of Supply Chain Stretch

Orchestration for any given business organization is the rearrangement, reconfiguring, and splicing together of various components of that organization into a cohesive design for the benefit of customers, suppliers, partners, and employees. As long as the status quo for a business remains intact, most modern businesses are organized to function smoothly. But what happens when a monkey wrench is thrown into the mix, affecting an organization's ability to make music or widgets as it did in the past? This not-altogether-unique and unplanned phenomenon of change being introduced into a company's established, systematized way of doing business is what we term "stretch." The ability of a company to adjust to that change and how it makes the adjustment is what we term "orchestration."

"Orchestrating stretch" requires a company to demand a performance at a whole new level. Imagine that a company is faced with an unforeseen chain of events that presents a significant opportunity for growth and development that, if executed correctly, will stretch the company's capabilities to such an extent that it will leave its competitors in the dust. Such opportunities may arise from new product successes, competitor failures, green product regulations, humanitarian logistics demands, product recalls, customized channels, mergers or acquisitions, and so on. If a company can orchestrate its capabilities to perform, then stretch opportunities convert to profitable execution and financial success.

We posit that to orchestrate stretch performance, the following capabilities have to be developed: (a) *flexibility*, that is, the ability to plug in and adapt to changes in the product mix; (b) *agility*, that is, the ability to reconfigure capacity across the supply chain to respond to demand-level changes; and (c) a portfolio of *real options* that offer the ability to exercise choices upon detection of shifts in demand or product types.

The cases in this book are outstanding examples of orchestration of stretch opportunities. In the Amazon.com example, growth at exceptional rates provided a challenge. The Amazon.com supply chains had to be designed to flex to accommodate product variety, resource surprises, and lead-time promises at a pace never before achieved. If such performance needs had not been anticipated, it is doubtful that Amazon.com's supply chain would have risen to the challenge. The secret to this performance is carefully designed agility, flexibility, and real options and an organization with the antennae to detect and adapt to shifts. Cross-training, esprit de corps, bins that can accommodate variety, mezzanine floors that can provide expanded storage, software that can reallocate orders and effectively estimate delivery performance, decision processes that can identify how best to use available delivery choices to provide promised performance at low cost, and finally a "carpe diem" attitude best represented by the CEO, Jeff Bezo, all combined to synchronize supply chain performance with business expectations. Remember how jazz performers synchronize their melodies? We submit that Amazon.com transformed a cacophony of disjointed supply chain pieces into a harmonious ensemble so that a buyer's click could initiate a seamless delivery performance by the supply chain.

The U.S. Coast Guard's performance during Hurricane Katrina shows another organization performing spectacularly in the face of mounting odds. With flooded streets, broken levees, downed communications, displaced people, and an overwhelmed civic system, what could the U.S. Coast Guard achieve? As the Government Accountability Office report suggests, they can achieve a lot. Assisting 1 year's worth of rescues in 10 days, redeploying personnel and aircraft across 26 air stations, prioritizing tasks at air stations to accommodate the surge from hurricane tasks, creating teams with members drawn across the organization, and providing decision-making authority to the level closest to the problem were all achievements recognized in the media. Equally important is the fact that this performance used existing protocols and procedures and represented a challenge for which the U.S. Coast Guard was well suited. Thus learning about the Coast Guard's capability allows one to understand how to cultivate the seeds that enable such performance. Again, the flexibility, agility, and real options as well as the decision-making authority to recognize how best to deploy resources, were all key ingredients to their success.

The Reflect.com example shows how to develop a unique supply chain within a large organization (Procter & Gamble [P&G]) that can enable customized beauty-care solutions. But how do you develop the capability by using plug-and-play capabilities across existing providers while keeping the overall capabilities a secret? Slivering the supply chain into carefully crafted individual tasks outsourced to best-of-breed performers, using P&G's research capability to develop fast approaches to create customized solutions, crafting warehousing and delivery solutions that leverage "on-demand" performance solutions from call centers to customer service to warehousing, and finally, developing a custom front end to extract customer preferences that best match customer product features all contributed to Reflect.com's performance. Every one of these steps provided flexibility and agility (by defining the custom products) and real options (by buying pay-for-performance solutions).

The Kryptonite lock case is a prime example of demand that was upturned overnight. Who would have thought that a 30-year-old product with guaranteed performance could be upended by a Bic pen and a YouTube video coupled with bloggers who spread the story? Can bloggers flay a product? Should companies develop the antennae to monitor blogger complaints about products so as to have advance warnings of product shortcomings? And when such data appeared, how did Kryptonite react? As the case describes, the company responded spectacularly with a commitment to customer service that took ownership of the product shortcomings and guaranteed replacement of products purchased over a 10-year period. Equally astonishing was a supply chain that replaced all products seamlessly. How many companies can expect such product surprises? Think about product recalls, contaminated inputs, and toy design flaws and suddenly Kryptonite experiences a potential performance challenge for all its products. Clearly the supply chain's product flexibility, agility, and the radar to identify and correct product shortcomings provided the operational performance to deal with this stretch opportunity, enabling the company to survive.

How will all U.S. households become net-zero energy consumers by 2020? Not without significant changes to every individual household—think roof tiles, heating and cooling equipment, dishwashers, washers and dryers, electronic equipment, light bulbs, recycling, and composting. All changes will have to be adopted by residential consumers. If the Department of Energy has its way, individual mandated changes will be the norm. Changes to the supply chain forced by the 2006 mandates on air-conditioning equipment provides an excellent example of the "opportunity" offered to distributors in this industry. Some large distributors, like Watsco, performed with flying colors. As the data show, anticipated potential supply glitches required them to use the inventory of the phased-out product as a real option. Flexible planning across their disparate regional companies enabled shared use of available inventory. Observed demand off-take based on regional inspection codes enabled redeployment of inventory. Adaptation to regional utility promotions of conservation enabled effective phase in of different manufacturer stock-keeping units (SKUs). All in all, tightly controlled planning and execution enabled the inventory's real option to be leveraged for optimal performance.

Behind every company with its multitude of transactions is an information system. An inflexible information system can surely hamper attempts to steer a company through choppy waters. BASF's use of SAP to provide phased management of their chemicals on ships headed to the Gulf during Hurricane Katrina and the planned deployment of all the cargo to alternate ports and handling agents provides one such example. Pharmaceutical companies' management of rollouts of products and their awareness of competitor actions, regulator responses to performance data, and so on suggest that supply chain event management may well become the norm. At the same time, SAP's reconfigurable software enables an event-management approach to software design that suggests the need to manage the information system as a response to management plans developed to weather potential contingencies in either demand or supply. Similarly, Shipwire's capability to manage logistics in the face of increasing demand from individual users allows the company to provide an outsourced model to handle stretch.

Humanitarian logistics contexts provide a sandbox to study approaches to management of stretch opportunities. After all, catastrophes appear with little or no warning, require immense coordination, demand scrambling to share capacity, and require prioritizing across competing goals while respecting norms and delivering against performance standards.

Often the agencies that operate in such environments look back on "lessons learned" and devise templates to deal with different contexts. We used operational deployment choices to suggest ways to orchestrate stretch goals.

In almost any business, there are fleeting opportunities that provide significant upsides. The challenge is to capitalize on these opportunities through the seamless execution and scaling of the supply chain. A common thread across all the examples and suggestions is the role of FAR—flexibility, agility, and real options in the supply chain. We believe that the concept of FAR can enable supply chains to capitalize on stretch opportunities efficiently. Enjoy the ride!

CHAPTER 13

A Stretchable Supply Chain Checklist

Questions All Managers Should Ask About Their Supply Chains

So how do you assess your company's ability to orchestrate stretch goals? We suggest that your answers to the following questions will provide you with an inventory of existing capabilities and, coupled with the ideas in this book, will suggest ways to move forward.

1. What are some of the *significant opportunities* that may arise in the future for your business in the areas of product changes, technology shifts, regulatory changes, new market opportunities, and so on?

2. How many *different supply chain configurations* can your company operate with existing assets, and how different are they from each other? Are your information systems set up to facilitate switching between configurations? How long would it take to accomplish these switches so that transactions are consistent and execution remains seamless from a customer perspective?

3. How does your company detect *changes in the business environment* and upside capabilities (organizationally)? How quickly can you switch between configurations, and how can you determine this switch (organizationally)? How are your incentives structured with respect to encouraging your employees to identify and manage upside opportunities? What checks and balances do you have to choose these opportunities and make sure they are consistent with your company's risk profile?

4. What *options* do you have with the supply base and the demand base to manage your business in the face of disruptive changes? How do

you manage the release of resources (money in particular) to manage upside opportunities?

5. How has *globalization* of your company and suppliers provided new occasions to manage upside opportunities?

Notes

Preface

1. Colvin, G. (2006, December 11). C-suite strategies: Q&A: On the hot seat. *Fortune*. Retrieved on January 21, 2011, from http://money.cnn.com/magazines/fortune/fortune_archive/2006/12/11/8395440/index.htm

2. Hamm, S., & Symonds, W. C. (2007, September 14). Kodak: Mistakes made on the road to innovation. *Bloomberg/BusinessWeek*. Retrieved on January 21, 2011, from http://www.businessweek.com/managing/content/sep2007/ca20070914_960180.htm

3. Reingold, J. (2009, January 22). Jim Collins: How great companies turn crisis into opportunity. *Fortune*. Retrieved on January 21, 2011, from http://money.cnn.com/2009/01/15/news/companies/Jim_Collins_Crisis.fortune/index.htm

4. Goldratt, E. M. (2004). *The goal: A process of ongoing improvement* (rev. ed.). Great Barrington, MA: North River Press.

Introduction

1. Palmisano, S. (2006, May–June). The globally integrated enterprise. *Foreign Affairs*. Retrieved on January 26, 2011, from http://www.foreignaffairs.com/articles/61713/samuel-j-palmisano/the-globally-integrated-enterprise

Chapter 1

1. Quote from Mr. Jeff Bezos, made during an all-employee meeting attended by Alex Zelikovsky.

2. Quote from Mr. Jimmy Wright, made during a planning meeting with Mr. Jeff Bezos and attended by Alex Zelikovsky.

3. Employees received company stock options as part of their compensation package.

Chapter 2

1. Horner, P., & List, B. (2010, September 7). Q&A: Admiral Mike Mullen: Armed with analytics. *Analytics*. Retrieved from http://analytics-magazine.com/?p=1374

2. Ripley, A. (2005, October 23). Hurricane Katrina: How the Coast Guard gets it right. *Time*. Retrieved from http://www.time.com/time/magazine/article/0,9171,1122007,00.html

3. U.S. General Accounting Office. (2006, July). *Coast Guard: Observations on the preparation, response, and recovery missions related to Hurricane Katrina*. Report no. GAO-06-903. Washington, DC: Author.

4. U.S. General Accounting Office. (2006, July). *Report to congressional committees: Coast Guard: Observations on the preparation, response, and recovery missions related to Hurricane Katrina* (Report no. 06-903). Washington, DC: Author. Retrieved from http://www.gao.gov/new.items/d06903.pdf

4. Ripley (2005).

5. Leonard, D. (2005, October 3). The only lifeline was the Wal-Mart. *Fortune*. Retrieved on January 21, 2011, from http://money.cnn.com/magazines/fortune/fortune_archive/2005/10/03/8356743/index.htm

6. Barbaro, M., & Gillis, J. (2005, September 6). Wal-Mart at forefront of hurricane relief. *Washington Post*. Retrieved from http://www.washingtonpost.com/wp-dyn/content/article/2005/09/05/AR2005090501598.html

7. Horowitz, S. (2009, August). Doing the right thing: The private sector response to Hurricane Katrina as a case study in bourgeois values. Working paper no. 09-33. Retrieved from http://mercatus.org/sites/default/files/publication/WP0933_Hurricane%20Katrina%20and%20the%20Bourgeois%20Virtues.pdf

8. Rosegrant, S. (2007). *Wal-Mart's response to Hurricane Katrina: Striving for a public-private partnership* (The Kennedy School of Government Case Program C16-07-1876.0). Cambridge, MA: Kennedy School of Government Case Studies in Public Policy & Management.

9. Walmartstores.com. (n.d.). Media information: Wal-Mart's response to Hurrican Katrina. *Walmart Corporate*. Retrieved from http://walmartstores.com/pressroom/news/5360.aspx

Chapter 3

1. Interview with Alex Zelikovsky. Quotes from Alex Zelikovsky.

Chapter 4

1. *Miami Herald*. (2006, June 6). A/C profit booming under new guidelines.

Chapter 5

1. See "Lorax." (2010, November 20). Kryptonite New York Fahgettaboutit Mini Bicycle U-Lock review: The best bike lock on the market. *Best Bike Lock*. Retrieved on January 26, 2011, from http://www.bestbikelock.net

2. Clark, J. S. (1992, October). D-brief: Forcing the security issue. *New Cyclist*. Retrieved on January 26, 2011, from http://www.brickbats.co.uk/D-locks.pdf

3. Kahney, L. (2004, September 14). Twist a pen, open a lock. *Wired*. Retrieved from http://www.wired.com/culture/lifestyle/news/2004/09/64987

4. Polgreen, L. (2004, September 17). The pen is mightier than the lock: A ballpoint trick infuriates bicyclists. *New York Times*. Retrieved from http://query.nytimes.com/gst/fullpage.html?res=9D03E0D71639F934A2575AC0A9629C8B63

5. Kirkpatrick, D. (2005, January 10). Why there is no escaping the blog. *Fortune*. Retrieved from http://money.cnn.com/magazines/fortune/fortune_archive/2005/01/10/8230982/index.htm

6. Kirkpatrick (2005).

7. Ochman, B. L. (2007, July 28). Kryptonite Lock: You've (ever so slowly) come a long way baby! *BL Ochman's Whatsnextblog*. Retrieved on January 26, 2011, from http://www.whatsnextblog.com/2007/07/in_2004_the_kryptonite_lock

Chapter 6

1. Tomasini, R., & Van Wassenhove, L. (2005). *Managing information in humanitarian crises: The UNJLC website*. (INSEAD case 04/2005-5278). New York, NY: INSEAD.

2. Iyer, A. V., & Van Wassenhove, L. (2004). Humanitarian logistics. Working paper.

Chapter 7

1. Crocs.com. (2010). Frequently asked questions. Retrieved from http://www.crocs.com.hk/faq/customer-service-faq,en_HK,pg.html

2. Markels, A. (2007, September 16). Croc and roll. *U.S. News*. Retrieved from http://money.usnews.com/money/business-economy/articles/2007/09/16/maker-of-popular-funky-crocs-footwear-is-on-the-hunt-for-its-next-big-hit.html

3. Gladwell, M. (2002). *The tipping point: How little things can make a big difference*. New York, NY: Back Bay Books.

4. See for more details Mucklehen.com. (2008, June 4). Has HD hit a "tipping point"? *The Muckle Hen's Scratchings*. Retrieved from http://blog.mucklehen.com/2008/06/04/has-hd-hit-a-tipping-point

5. Associated Press. (2008, April 19). Japan asks Crocs for a redesign. *Washington Post*. Retrieved from http://www.washingtonpost.com/wp-dyn/content/article/2008/04/18/AR2008041803068.html

6. Marzulli, J. (2008, February 7). Suit: Crocs shoe led to 3-year-old girl's toe accident on JFK escalator. *New York Daily News*. Retrieved from http://www.nydailynews.com/news/2008/02/07/2008-02-07_suit_crocs_shoe_led_to_3yearold_girls_to-2.html

7. Fabregas, L. (2007, July 31). Mercy Hospital goes on a Crocs hunt. *Pittsburgh Tribune-Review*. Retrieved from http://www.pittsburghlive.com/x/pittsburghtrib/news/cityregion/s_519819.html

8. Associated Press. (2007, April 20). Crocs a fashion faux pas for doctors. Retrieved from http://www.msnbc.msn.com/id/18233132/ns/health-health_care

9. Tirrel, M., & Timberlake, C. (2008, July 25). Crocs sinks on concern allure is fading as sales drops. *Bloomberg*. Retrieved from http://www.bloomberg.com/apps/news?pid=newsarchive&sid=asRJq93MQUDo

10. Andrejczac, M. (2010, September 28). Crocs shares are back in fashion. *The Wall Street Journal MarketWatch*. Retrieved from http://www.marketwatch.com/story/crocs-shares-are-back-in-fashion-2010-09-28

Chapter 8

1. Alex Zelikovsky's discussions with senior managers from FreeFlow were background sources for this chapter.

2. An "infomediary" is a service provider using technology or information to deliver value to a customer.

3. Freeflow. (n.d.). Background. *Freeflow.com*. Retrieved on January 26, 2011, from http://www.freeflow.com/about-us/background

4. FreeFlow. (2009). Cash in on at risk inventory. *Freeflow.com*. Retrieved on February 21, 2011, from http://www.freeflow.com/wp-content/uploads/2010/02/at-risk.pdf

Chapter 9

1. SAP. (2006). SAP customer success story: Chemicals. Retrived from http://www.sap.com/industries/chemicals/pdf/CS_BASF.pdf

2. Alex Zelikovsky's discussions with a senior manager at SAP.

3. "Batch" is an economic production quantity.

4. "Lot size" is the level of inventory that minimizes the total inventory holding and ordering costs.

5. Sap.com. (n.d.). SOA navigation. *SAP Help website*. Retrieved on January 26, 2011, from http://help.sap.com/content/documentation/esoa/docu_esoa_intro.htm

6. Something "modular" implies components that may be separated and recompiled into a more agile process.

7. Clancy, H. (2008, April). Shipping 2.0. *Entrepreneur*. Retrieved from http://www.entrepreneur.com/magazine/entrepreneur/2008/april/191638.html

Chapter 10

1. Jim Kagey, vice president of logistics at Henry Schein, phone interview with Ananth Iyer and Alex Zelikovsky.

2. "Split-case distribution" refers to direct-to-consumer distribution.

3. "Full-case distribution" refers to retail or business-to-business distribution.

4. "Off-line product handling" refers to large, bulky, or irregular shaped products that cannot be moved through regular automation processes within the distribution center.

Chapter 11

1. Palmisano, S. (2006, May–June). The globally integrated enterprise. *Foreign Affairs*. Retrieved on January 26, 2011, from http://www.foreignaffairs.com/articles/61713/samuel-j-palmisano/the-globally-integrated-enterprise.

Index

Announcing the Business Expert Press Digital Library

*Concise E-books Business Students Need
for Classroom and Research*

This book can also be purchased in an e-book collection by your library as

- a one-time purchase,
- that is owned forever,
- allows for simultaneous readers,
- has no restrictions on printing, and
- can be downloaded as PDFs from within the library community.

Our digital library collections are a great solution to beat the rising cost of textbooks. e-books can be loaded into their course management systems or onto student's e-book readers.

The **Business Expert Press** digital libraries are very affordable, with no obligation to buy in future years.

For more information, please visit **www.businessexpert.com/libraries**. To set up a trial in the United States, please contact **Sheri Allen** at *sheri.allen@globalepress.com*; for all other regions, contact **Nicole Lee** at *nicole.lee@igroupnet.com*.

OTHER TITLES IN OUR SUPPLY AND OPERATIONS
MANAGEMENT COLLECTION
Series Editor: **Steven Nahmias**

A Primer on Negotiating Corporate Purchase Contracts by Patrick Penfield

Production Line Efficiency: A Comprehensive Guide for Managers by Sabry Shaaban and Sarah Hudson

Transforming U.S. Army Supply Chains: Strategies for Management Innovation by Greg H. Parlier

Design, Analysis, and Optimization of Supply Chains: A System Dynamics Approach by William R. Killingsworth